82nd AIRBORNE
'All American'

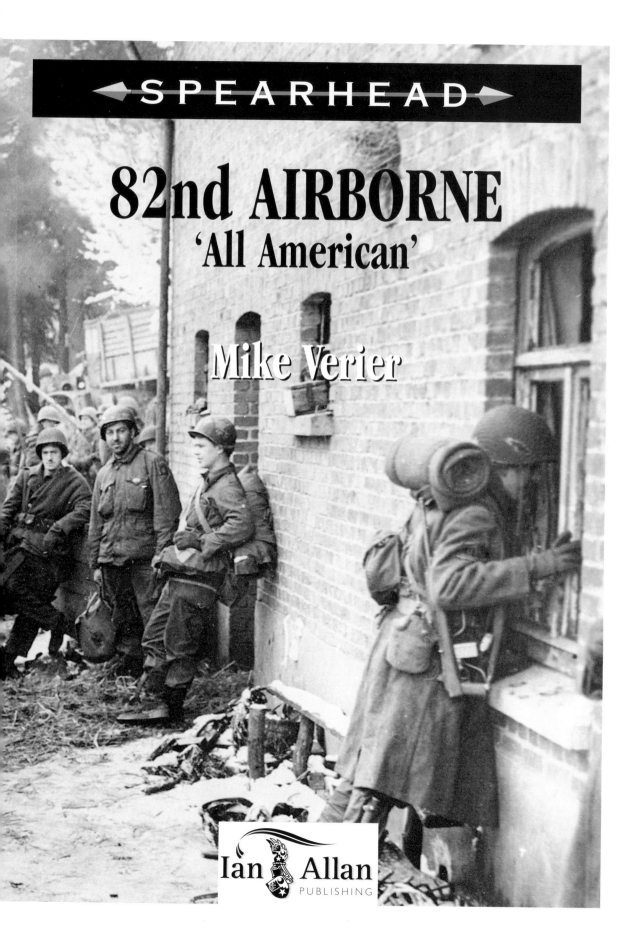

SPEARHEAD

82nd AIRBORNE
'All American'

Mike Verier

Ian Allan
PUBLISHING

First published 2001

ISBN 0 7110 2856 7

© Compendium Publishing 2001

Published by Ian Allan Publishing

an imprint of Ian Allan Publishing Ltd, Hersham, Surrey KT12 4RG.
Printed by Ian Allan Printing Ltd, Hersham, Surrey KT12 4RG.

Code: 0112/A2

British Library Cataloguing in Publication Data
A CIP catalogue record for this book is available from the British Library

Cover: 82nd Airborne re-enactors. (Tim Hawkins)

Previous page: Men of 508th PIR await orders, 6 January 1945. (via Real War Photos)

Abbreviations

AA(A)	Anti-aircraft artillery	Engr	Engineer	QM	Quartermaster
		ETO	European Theatre of Operations	Pfc/Pvt	Private (first class)
AB	Airborne			Pl	Platoon
ADC	Aide de camp	FA	Field Artillery	PIR	Parachute infantry regiment
Amb	Ambulance	GIR	Glider infantry regiment		
Arty	Artillery	gren	Grenade	Recce/Recon	Reconnaissance
asst	Assistant	HMG	Heavy MG (.50 cal)	RA	Royal Artillery
A/tk	Anti-tank			RCT	Regimental Combat Team
ATRL	Anti-tank rocket launcher (M6 Bazooka)	Hy	Heavy	RHQ	Regimental HQ
		Inf	Infantry	Sect	Section
Bn	Battalion	LMG	Light MG (.30 cal)	(T or S/) Sgt	(Technical or Staff/) Sergeant
BR	British	LST	Landing Ship Tank		
Brig	Brigade	Lt	light	SHAEF	Supreme HQ Allied Powers in Europe
Bty	Battery	(1-/2-)Lt	(First/Second) Lieutenant	Sig	Signals
camo	camouflage	LZ	Landing zone	SP	Self-propelled
Cav	Cavalry	Maint	Maintenance	Tac	Tactical
CC	Combat Command	MC	Motorcycle	Tk	Tank
C-in-C	Commander-in-Chief	Med	Medium or Medical	USAAF	US Army Air Force
Cml	Chemical			USMC	US Marine Corps
Col	Column	MG	Machine gun	Veh	Vehicle
Coy	Company	Mor	Mortar		
Det	Detachment	Mot Inf	Motorised infantry	**Dates**	
DZ	Dropzone	MP	Military Police	20/7/54	20 July 1954
ea	each	Mtrel	Materiel		

CONTENTS

Acknowledgements

As ever the production of a book like this is not a solo effort, many people gave of their time and expertise that it might have life. I should particularly like to record the efforts of Bob Anzuoni at the 82nd Division Museum, Fort Bragg, and Patrick Tremblay at the Airborne and Special Operations Museum, Fayetteville. Both assisted with research and answered strange questions in the middle of the night. Bob made his archive freely available to me whilst the other members of the museum staff willingly put up with a visiting Brit for several days.

My latest visit to Bragg was greatly assisted by Major Randy Martin and colleagues of the XVIII th Airborne Corps, and the staff of the 82nd PAO—special thanks here to Sgt Christina Bhatti. As ever the men and women of the 82nd made me welcome wherever I went.

On this side of the Atlantic Col. Derek Armitage and his staff at the Museum of Army flying also made their archive available and helped with photographs at very short notice. Others include Joe Murchison of the Triple Nickles, my good friend Lt.Col Peyton DeHart USMC (not forgetting Jane, Bill and Cathy Johnson and Mike Brady of the Army Aviation Heritage Foundation). Technical support for which I am eternally grateful, was provided by Wendy Ash and Sarah Ross, whilst photographic assistance came from Canterbury Camera Centre.

My thanks go to Chris Ellis, George Forty, Simon Forty and Bruce Robertson for some of the information and many of the illustrations used in this book. The maps on page 64 are based on two in Robert Kershaw's excellent *D-Day* (Ian Allan Ltd, 1985). Frank Ainscough designed the book; Donald Sommerville edited it; Mark Franklin of Flatt Art did the maps.
Airborne!

Mike Verier July 2001

ORIGINS & HISTORY

First activated at Camp Gordon, Georgia, on 25 August 1917, scarcely four months after the USA had entered World War I, the 82nd Division was part of the National Army (the term used in WWI to describe drafted soldiers). It drew its original complement of conscripts from states such as Alabama, Georgia and Tennessee. First commanded by Major General Eben Swift, the division's 28,000 men (authorised strength was 991 officers and 27,114 other ranks) soon came to include soldiers from every state of the Union (not to mention that some 20% of inductees proved to be of foreign birth). Once this was realised the name 'All American' was chosen and the red, white and blue 'double A' insignia adopted.

The US was committed to a goal of 'one million men in France by May 1918' and such massive expansion inevitably led to equipment shortages in the short term, In the early stages at least the division was forced to train with wooden rifles. British and French officers with experience in trench warfare were seconded to provide first-hand guidance and training which greatly aided the process. Shortages of grenades and machine guns led to something of an emphasis on the bayonet—which may account for the aggressive reputation the unit subsequently acquired in France.

FRANCE

By early 1918 the division was deemed combat ready, and in April that year embarked for France under the command of Major General William P. Burnham, the second National Army unit so to do. Deployment in 1918 was by sea, and the men of the 82nd were doubtless somewhat relieved to land briefly in England after the long Atlantic crossing. The brevity of their passage onward to Le Havre did not prevent a regiment of the division (the 325th Infantry) from becoming the first American unit to be reviewed by King George V as it marched past Buckingham Palace. In later years reviews were to become something of a speciality when the division was not in combat, but for now there was a war to be got on with.

Combat

On arrival in France the division prepared itself for action, moving up to the line by rail on 16 June from its initial training area near the Somme. As this first deployment was in a French sector the troops were issued with French weapons, including Chauchat and Hotchkiss machine guns, in order to make resupply easier. On 25 June 1918 the All American Division saw combat for the first time, near the city of Toul in the Lagny sector of northeastern France, its assignment being to relieve the 26th Division.

Men of the division had in fact been in the front line prior to this. Officers and NCOs had gained some combat experience with the British on the Somme sector whilst the bulk of the division was working up. The unfortunate distinction of being the 82's first casualty had fallen to Captain Jewitt Williams of the 326th Infantry Regiment, who was killed on 9 June.

The first full battalions into the front line trenches were the 2nd/325th, 1st/326th, 3rd/327th, and 2nd/328th. As the 82nd's artillery units were still training, artillery support was provided by the French. By mid-July the division's own machine-gun units had joined the infantry, and on 4 August the first night raid was mounted. Companies K and M of the 326th Infantry, supported by the 320th Machine Gun Battalion, attacked German positions at Flirey, penetrating some 600 yards. By the time the division was moved out of the sector on 10 August it had already suffered 374 casualties.

Respite was brief, the 82nd relieving the 2nd Division in the Marbache sector on 15 August. Finally, its own artillery joined up in the shape of the 157th Artillery Brigade. Supposedly a quiet sector, Marbache was in fact far from restful, artillery bombardment and strafing from the air alternating with aggressive German patrolling.

The first major American offensive of the war, the St Mihiel offensive, was to see the 82nd assigned the village of Norroy as an objective on 12 September. The capture of this was reported as 'relatively easy', although the division suffered 950 casualties during the offensive. One of the 78 killed was the 82nd's first Medal of Honor winner, Lt Colonel Emory Pike. The division was in action until 17 September when it was once again stationed in the Marbache sector, moving on the 20th to prepare for its part in the Meuse-Argonne offensive. The St Mihiel offensive ended on 21 September.

Above: Observation post on the Western Front. (82nd Airborne Museum)

The Meuse-Argonne Offensive

The division was moved to the Clermont area west of Verdun on 24 September to act as reserve for the US First Army. The offensive began on the 26th and on the 29th the 327th Infantry Regiment was committed, at 90 minutes' notice, to bolster the line near Apremont. The regiment force-marched to its positions and held them against strong German attacks until relieved two days later by the 1st Division.

The rest of the division joined the 327th near Varennes on 4 October, and two days later the 82nd moved back into the front line, relieving the 28th Division. Also on the 4th Major General George P. Duncan took command of the All Americans, relieving William P. Burnham (by then a brigadier general).

The division's 164th Brigade was back on the offensive on 7 October, wresting Hills 180 and 223 from the Germans. It was during this action that Alvin York, a former conscientious objector from Tennessee, was to win the divisions' second Medal of Honor and become possibly the most famous American soldier of the war.

Further regiments of the 82nd attacked northwards on 10 October, forcing the Germans from the eastern half of the Argonne Forest. The ground they gained was held for three weeks until the 77th and 80th Divisions relieved the division and continued the offensive.

The 82nd had earned an impressive reputation during the Meuse-Argonne offensive. It had cost the division dear, however, with over 6,000 casualties, including 902 killed. This perhaps was the earliest example for the 82nd of a

Below: 325th Infantry parade in front of Buckingham Palace, London in 1918 reviewed by King George V and the dowager Princess Alexandra. (82nd Airborne Museum)

Left: Ammo dump in France. (82nd Airborne Museum)

problem common to all good military formations, 'the better you are, the more work they give you'.

Some two weeks later came the eleventh hour, of the eleventh day, of the eleventh month, the Armistice.

The road home

The division spent the next three months near Pravthay where it continued to train whilst awaiting orders for home. At last on 2 March 1919 the 82nd began the move to Bordeaux and home. On arrival in New York the division was de-mobilised, de-activation being completed formally on 27 May 1919, the All American Division was to remain a slumbering giant for the next 23 years.

During America's brief involvement in the Great War the men of the 82nd had spent 105 days in the front lines and suffered 1,035 killed in action. A further 378 troopers would succumb to wounds received in combat before the final accounting. In addition to the two Medal of Honor winners, three soldiers of the 82nd won Distinguished Service Medals, and 75 the Distinguished Service Cross. Sergeant York also received the French Croix de Guerre with palm leaves and the Legion d'Honneur, the Italian Croce de Guerra, and the Montenegrin War Medal.

By June 1919 most of the soldiers had been discharged and were on their way back to civilian life. At that point the 82nd Division had passed into history. The flame, however, still flickered and from 1921 until World War II the 82nd Infantry Division, unaware of its destiny, was part of the organised reserves. Until 1942 a reserve HQ was at Columbia, South Carolina.

READY FOR WAR

Whilst the 82nd was slumbering, events in the rest of the world were moving inexorably towards another global conflict. In Germany the emergent military machine was of necessity starting from scratch. This meant that many new doctrines and ideas were embraced. The Germans were not alone in fielding airborne forces; both the Russians and the Italians had developed parachute infantry (the former specialising in what the 82nd now do best, the airfield take-down) but it was the Germans who refined the airborne concept and fully integrated it into their force structure. What the Russians regarded an aerial club hammer, the Germans developed into a rapier.

The Germans saw air power *per se* as an adjunct to the army, almost as long range artillery in fact, but they also recognised the inherent mobility that transport by air could impart. More to the point, they were determined not to get bogged down in the static warfare of WWI. The term Blitzkrieg (lightning war) was coined to describe the new strategy, a word the world was to come to know only too well. The idea was simple: instead of costly frontal assaults on heavily fortified positions, attrition warfare, they would simply go around them. In the case of line fortifications specialist shock troops would go over them, attack from the rear and open breaches for the heavy units to pour through. All this was made possible by the aeroplane.

The concept of airborne assault was not unique or original to Germany for as far back as 1784 Benjamin Franklin had correctly encapsulated the potential of airborne forces, though this potential was naturally unrealisable at the time as the means to transport them were not available. More realistically, in the closing months of World War I Billy Mitchell (who later also correctly prophesied the demise of battleships to air power) planned airborne assaults on Metz. These were more than mere ideas on the back of cigarette packets; the planning was detailed, thorough, and well advanced. The staff officer assigned to this task in 1918 by Mitchell was Lt Colonel Lewis Brereton, who 26 years later would command the First Allied Airborne Army during Operation Market-Garden. With the signing of the Armistice, however, American interest in developing new weapons and tactics ceased, was this not the war to end wars?

The development of General Kurt Student's *Fallschirmjäger* (literally 'hunters from the sky') is beyond the scope of this narrative. Their growth pre-war, and success in the early years was, however, watched keenly by military men of other nations who ultimately copied or adapted most of the German tactics and equipment.* Not least amongst these was one Major William C. Lee, a former infantry officer sent to Germany by Chief of Infantry Major General George Lynch as an observer.

*The replication of German equipment was quite thorough (why waste good development?) the jump smock and cut-down helmet being copied almost exactly by the British as were the containers for heavy weapons and ammunition. The similarity between the two forces was such that it later led to some difficulty in telling the two apart once covered in the dust of war. The US airborne forces for their part tried to adapt standard issue items where they could, albeit using the German model as their guide. One item they did take on board, however, (and eventually make their own) was the jump boot.

THE CONCEPT DEVELOPS

Above: The first stages of jump conditioning came from training at Camp Toccoa, Georgia. (via Bruce Robertson)

Interest in the use of airborne troops was lukewarm in America during the 1930s. There were studies of course, and the usual inter-service rivalry about who should 'own' the soldiers. Claimants included the Engineers, because demolition would be a major role, the Infantry (who eventually won) because once on the ground they would fight as infantry, and the Air Corps who felt that the proposed 'air infantry' unit should be subordinate to it (like the Marines were and still are to the Navy) because it provided the aircraft. Unfortunately, as there were never enough aircraft available, the whole idea was shelved.

Lee meanwhile, returned to the US full of enthusiasm for the development of airborne forces. Serving on Lynch's staff in Washington, DC, he was well placed to lobby those that mattered. His enthusiasm paid off when, in 1940, with most of Europe already overwhelmed by Blitzkrieg tactics, President Roosevelt personally directed that priority be given to the development of airborne (glider and parachute) forces. This was the moment of conception for the Airborne, and the gestation period that followed was to be short.

In February 1940 development of a suitable parachute began at Wright Field, Ohio. The Infantry Board directed that this be accomplished as soon as possible, and that a volunteer unit be formed to test it. The resultant T4 static line 'chute was ready by 25 June when Major Lee was authorised to seek volunteers from the 29th Infantry Regiment (a demonstration unit for the Infantry School). The following month 'Hap' Arnold of the Air Corps also initiated full-scale development of suitable gliders, four companies vying for contracts to develop a suitable aircraft. In May the Fallschirmjäger demonstrated what paratroopers and gliders could do in Holland and at Fort Eben Emael in Belgium.

The test platoon

Authorised on 25 June 1940, the Parachute Test Platoon was formed at Fort Benning in July under the command of Lieutenant William T. Ryder. It consisted of 48 hand-picked men selected from numerous volunteers* (there were actually 39 enlisted slots, but the high possibility of injury was taken into account). Its mission was to develop and test equipment, tactics and training methods that would enable the fielding of parachute troops. The men set to with a will.

During the next eight weeks, with France surrendered and the Battle of Britain raging (and the very real prospect of Britain also falling to the Nazis) the men of the Test Platoon trained hard. The programme included physical fitness training, landing techniques, tactics, and tower jumps (which were carried out at a civilian facility near New York, the troopers spending some ten days at Fort Dix). During at least one of the tower jumps General Lynch came from Washington to jump with the men—a firm precedent. The platoon also tested various weapons, items of clothing and equipment, including modified baseball helmets, which were used initially for all jumps. The culmination of the course was to be five live jumps that would qualify the men as parachutists. On 16 August Lieutenant Ryder, leading from the front (as would become standard practice in the Airborne) duly became the US Army's first paratrooper.

Prophetically this first jump was made (reportedly) from a 'C-33'. This was a military version of a revolutionary aircraft for its time, the Douglas DC-2. Very few of these were delivered to the Air Corps because the basic aircraft rapidly evolved into the more capable—and infinitely more famous—DC-3/C-47 Dakota, an aircraft that was to become as familiar to the paratroopers of WWII as the Huey helicopter became to the Vietnam generation.

The last of the five jumps was carried out before an audience heavy with brass (including the Secretary for War and several generals) and took the form of a mock assault. It is not recorded if the 'howling' troopers that so impressed them with the efficiency and ferocity of their assault could actually be heard bawling 'Geronimo!' as they left the aircraft, another tradition begun with the platoon.

Things now moved into high gear. The Test Platoon formed the cadre of the training school that Benning was to become as the first full battalion (the 501st

Some 200 enlisted men and 17 lieutenants volunteered for the Test Platoon, despite the Army's frank admission that the job would require 'frequent jumps from airplanes, which may result in serious injury or death' and a consequent insistence on unmarried soldiers only.

Below: Jump towers were used for training. (via Bruce Robertson)

Parachute Infantry) was authorised by the War Department. By November 1940 three more battalions had been authorised, as well as the first uniform distinctions. The troopers were permitted to blouse (or tuck) their trousers into their boots and wear the overseas cap with parachute insignia. Shortly after Bill Yarborough (while a lieutenant) was to design the distinctive jump wings. (He later went on to develop the M1941 Airborne Field Uniform and the coveted jump boots. See page 87.)

On 20 May 1941, whilst America was just beginning to form the basis of a parachute arm, the cloudless blue sky over Crete was reverberating to the sound of Junkers Ju52 tri-motors. Gliders and paratroopers filled the sky, another powerful demonstration of air assault was underway. Whilst the Germans were successful in their assault on Crete the price was high, the unsupported paratroopers suffering the loss of nearly half their number in the initial assault. Ironically, therefore, whilst Crete galvanised America's development of an airborne force, it actually marked the end (on Hitler's personal order) of large scale assault operations by the *Fallschirmjäger*.

During the next few months, training and the development of gliders proceeded ever more urgently. The 502nd and 503rd Battalions were activated in July and August respectively and the Waco CG-4A glider was chosen for full-scale production.

Initially some 150 pilots were trained to form the initial glider units. On a peace-time basis this would probably have sufficed—America was still trying to keep out of the 'European War'—but then came 7 December 1941, Pearl Harbor, and America was at war.

On 20 December the pilot requirement was increased to 1,000, by April 1942 it had risen to 4,200, and then later to 6,000. Even by scouring draftees for anyone with experience, asking for volunteers and training at civilian schools the demand could not be met. Qualifications were ultimately reduced to the most rudimentary (presumably on the basis that a good landing is 'one you walk away from' and that one good landing would therefore be enough). In fact this shortage was never really overcome. By the time of the Arnhem operations it was common practice for the senior NCO present in a glider to be 'promoted' to co-pilot during the flight to the landing zone. He would thus spend his hour or so bumping along in the slipstream of the towing Dakota being instructed on the basics of landing the thing should the pilot be incapacitated.

In January 1942 the War Department directed that four regiments be formed as the nucleus of Airborne Command. At that time a parachute regiment consisted of three battalions with a total of 1,958 men. In March the now Colonel Lee received his official orders from General Leslie McNair to activate the Command. Lee knew that the burgeoning operation would soon outgrow the facilities at Fort Benning, and began the move to Fort Bragg, North Carolina, where there was vastly more room.

Above: Helmet at a rakish angle, this early war photograph shows a parade-ground para. The weapon is a folding-stock carbine, specially developed for airborne troops; it was not widely used.

REACTIVATION

At the same time all the whole US Army was expanding and moving to a war footing. As part of this rapid expansion the 82nd Infantry Division was reactivated at Camp Claiborne, Louisiana, under Major General Omar Bradley. It was 23 March 1942 and training commenced immediately.

As the 82nd and other infantry divisions got down to hard training the fledgling airborne force continued to expand. In May the first glider regiment, the 88th Glider Infantry Regiment (GIR), came into being, equipped with CG-4s. Through the summer experiments continued with a view to providing artillery for the airborne. Initially these centred on the 75mm pack-howitzer, which was designed to be broken down into mule loads and thus thought ideal for air-dropping.*

Bradley meanwhile had been bringing his command to a high degree of proficiency but was then transferred away. On 15 August the War Department designated the 82nd Infantry as America's first airborne division. Half its manpower was to form the second, the 101st 'Screaming Eagles', with Lee in command. Bradley's deputy, Ridgway, assumed command of the 82nd. Intensive training for the 82nd continued at Camp Claiborne until, on 1 October, it moved to Bragg, destined to be its home to this day.

Training, organisation and doctrine

Apart from the obvious need to train soldiers in parachuting, the new division worked to develop tactics that would best suit its intended role—best summarised as 'assault troops'. The classic use of paratroops, as so ably demonstrated in the Low Countries, is a surprise attack behind an enemy's front line, to take and hold key features such as bridges, eliminate defensive structures and sabotage communications, thus opening the way for supporting heavier forces, which can then exploit the breach.

By definition, paratroops are infantry and therefore lightly armed, though this is a relative term as 'lightly' is not quite the word that comes to mind on seeing pictures of troopers festooned with seemingly their own body weight in weapons, equipment and ammunition. The technology of the time did not allow for precise insertion of units and a pragmatic assumption was made that the lightly equipped troopers would be frequently engaged in small-unit actions. This meant that they were going to have to be self-sufficient and capable of operating on their own initiative almost down to individual level. Paratroopers expected to be unsupported in the initial phase of an attack. Depending on how far from the front line they were, this could be for days.

Such a scenario demanded much of the soldiers individually, and was the reason why only above-average candidates were recruited. A paratrooper, by the nature of his job, was going to need to be intelligent, physically fit, motivated, highly trained and absolutely confident in the abilities both of his officers and his fellow troopers.

The 82nd was selected to convert to this new role because it was considered to be all these things. Bradley had melded the All Americans into a fine fighting force that already possessed a strong sense of identity, and high motivation (there exists a set of grainy pictures showing Bradley and Ridgway tackling the assault course at Claiborne with obvious gusto—no leading from a desk for Airborne generals). All that remained was to turn infantrymen into paratroops or glider-borne soldiers.

At Benning the basic course for paratroops lasted four weeks. The first week was about assessing fitness, with gruelling physical tests and lots of running. This phase varied depending on the quality of the troops, and was sometimes skipped if the incoming soldiers were sufficiently fit. Famously, the men of one of the earliest intakes, the 506th (later to be assigned to the 101st) were so fit that they left their instructors standing. After two days of being thus humiliated the sergeants gave in and moved their charges to the next stage.

The second week still featured the press-ups and the running but this time to the packing sheds where the troopers learnt how to pack their 'chutes. With their lives literally depending on it, folding, packing and checking became second nature. This was interspersed with learning how to exit the aircraft and land properly.

This phase used mock-up fuselages, mounted a few feet above a sand pit. Even at this early stage training was designed to ensure that the men would actually jump when the moment came. They were instructed to look straight out at the horizon—

not down—an obvious enough technique, and more subtly they were drilled to place their hands on the outside of the door when preparing for the jump. This meant that they could not easily resist jumping. The instructors knew that, if a man steadied himself with his hands on the inside of the door and then 'froze', nothing, including the weight of the men behind him, could force him out quickly. Usually the second week also included tower jumps in harnesses attached to steel cables, again this was to work on the landing technique. The third week moved the troopers on to 'free' jumps in parachutes dropped from 250ft towers, with at least one of these jumps at night. Benning also possessed a wind machine to train the men in how to collapse the canopy and avoid being dragged after landing.

The culmination of all this training was the fourth week. Five true jumps would earn the men their wings, and by now they were at peak preparedness, psychologically and physically. The enormity of the first jump should not be underestimated. In the 1940s most of the enlisted men had never even been in an aeroplane and so their first jump was also their first flight, something easily forgotten some 60 years on when air travel is commonplace and casual.

Much time was expended the night before the jump. Parachutes were packed, checked and re-packed. The following morning the troopers double-marched to Benning's Lawson Field and were divided into groups of 24 to await their introduction to the C-47. Once airborne the Dakotas climbed to 1,500ft to begin the drop. On the red light the jumpmasters gave the order 'Stand up and hook up' at which each man attached the snap-hook of his static line main parachute to a cable running the length of the cabin roof. Each trooper would check the next man's line and count off by number when all was secure.

Come the green light and the training usually took over. Each trooper, moving now automatically to the door, took up the jump position. The instructor would tap him on the leg and out he would go. Fifteen feet out of the door the static line pulled the back of the parachute pack open and the apex of the parachute out into the airflow. As it reached full extension a break-cord finally separated the soldier from the aircraft, the canopy blooming in the 120-knot slipstream of the departing Dakota. His headlong descent now suddenly slowed, the trooper had a few brief seconds to savour the exhilaration of the moment before preparing for landing. He had done it; he was going to be a paratrooper.

Four more jumps, the parade, the silver wings and the transition from 'legs' to paratrooper. At last allowed to blouse their trousers into their jump boots and wear the distinctions of the Airborne soldier, the newly qualified troopers were permitted a few days leave. Farm boys, college kids, garage mechanics, barmen or office workers when they left home, they all returned as paratroopers, they were now members of an élite.

When they returned to Benning it was not to the spartan wooden huts of the 'Frying Pan' training area, but across the river to rather more civilised accommodation. The training however continued relentlessly. Jumps with full kit and weapons, live training in small unit actions, practice assaults, night manoeuvres, and more weapon training. Things were hotting up and the rumour mills began to generate all sorts of stories about where they might be deployed.

Above: Training drop of troops and equipment containers (those with white 'chutes and single-point attachments). (via Chris Ellis)

82nd AIRBORNE DIVISION WARTIME UNITS

82nd Airborne Division fought under 10 Allied armies and 19 corps. The following subordinate units were permanently assigned to the division:

Div HQ and HQ Coy
82nd Airborne MP Platoon
325th Glider Infantry Regiment
504th Parachute Infantry Regiment
505th Parachute Infantry Regiment
HQ and HQ Battery Divisional Artillery
319th Glider Field Artillery Battalion

320th Glider Field Artillery Battalion
376th Parachute Field Artillery Battalion
456th Parachute Field Artillery Battalion
80th Airborne Anti-Aircraft Battalion
307th Airborne Engineer Battalion
407th Airborne Quartermaster Company
307th Airborne Medical Company
821st Airborne Signals Company
782nd Airborne Ordnance Maint Company
82nd Airborne Reconnaissance Platoon
82nd Parachute Maintenance Company

These units were attached to the 82nd for long periods of time and were considered vital parts of the division during the combat periods noted:

508th PIR	Normandy, Holland, Ardennes, Rhineland.
2nd Bn, 401st GIR	Normandy, Holland, Ardennes, Rhineland.
507th PIR	Normandy.
666th QM Truck Coy	Holland, Ardennes, Central Europe.

Attached units

The following units were attached to the division during the campaigns and at the dates indicated:

North Africa

Complete records of attachments in North Africa are not available but included the following:

2nd Bn, 509th Pl Engr Company (Cam) (sic)
334th QM Company (Depot)

Sicily

Complete records of attachments in Sicily. are not available but included the following:

39th Regimental Combat Team
26th Field Artillery Battalion
34th Field Artillery Battalion
62nd Field Artillery Battalion
77th Field Artillery Battalion
20th Engineer Battalion (C) (sic)
83rd Chemical Battalion (4.2-inch Mortar)

Italy

Complete records of attachments in Italy are not currently available but included the following:

3rd Ranger Battalion (to 504th Parachute RCT)
Gurkha Battalion (BR) (to 504th Parachute RCT) (sic)

England

Unit	From	To
Quartermaster Truck Coy	20/1/44	27/8/44
HQ and HQ Co, 2nd Airborne Brigade	20/1/44	27/8/44
507th Parachute Infantry Regt	20/1/44	27/8/44
508th Parachute Infantry Regt	20/1/44	30/3/45

Normandy

Unit	From	To
Troop B, 4th Cav Recon Sqn	1/6/44	23/6/44
87th Armored Field Artillery Bn	1/6/44	8/6/44
	1/6/44	8/7/44
Coy C, 746th Tank Bn	1/6/44	11/6/44
Coy A, 746th Tank Bn	13/6/44	21/6/44
Coy A, 712th Tank Bn	1/7/44	8/7/44
188th Field Artillery Bn	12/6/44	8/7/44
172nd Field Artillery Bn	16/6/44	19/6/44
Coy C, 899th TD Bn	1/6/44	19/6/44
Coy A, 607th TD Bn	19/6/44	4/7/44
801st Tank Destroyer Bn	30/6/44	1/7/44
803rd Tank Destroyer Bn	1/7/44	8/7/44
Coy B, 87th Chemical Mortar Bn	15/6/44	21/6/44
Coy D, 86th Chemical Mortar Bn	1/7/44	4/7/44
3809th QM Truck Coy		
3810th QM Truck Coy		
1st Platoon 603rd QM GR Coy		
1st Pl, 464th Amb Coy, 31st Med Group		
493rd Collecting Coy, 179th Med Bn		
374th Collecting Coy 50th Med Bn		
429th Litter Bearing Platoon		
591st Collecting Coy		

Holland

Unit	From	To
Unit A, 50th Field Hospital	17/9/44	
666th Quartermaster Truck Coy	19/9/44	
1st Coldstream Guards (BR)	19/9/44	22/9/44
5th Coldstream Guards (BR)	19/9/44	22/9/44
2nd Irish Guards (BR)	19/9/44	22/9/44
Sherwood Rangers Yeomanry (BR)	19/9/44	10/10/44
Royals Recce Bn (BR) (sic)	19/9/44	9/10/44
Polish Parachute Brigade	25/9/44	30/9/44
231st Brigade (BR)	30/9/44	1/10/44
3rd Guards Brigade (BR)	30/9/44	1/10/44
5th Coldstream Guards (BR)	30/9/44	10/10/44
79th Field Artillery Regt (BR) (sic)	30/9/44	2/10/44
304th Anti-tank Battery (BR) (sic)	30/9/44	3/10/44
506th Parachute Infantry Regt	1/10/44	3/10/44
502nd Parachute Infantry Regt	3/10/44	4/10/44

130th Infantry Brigade (BR)	5/10/44	6/10/44
2nd Grenadier Guards (BR)	6/10/44	7/10/44
13th/18th Hussars (BR)	10/10/44	10/11/44

Ardennes

Unit A, 50th Field Hospital		
666th Quartermaster Truck Coy		
Coy C, 563d AAA Bn	18/12/44	25/12/44
Combat Command B, 9th Armored Division	23/12/44	24/12/44
Coy B, 86th Chemical Bn	25/12/44	11/1/45
254th Field Artillery Bn	20/12/44	18/2/45
551st Parachute Infantry Bn	25/12/44	12/1/45
703rd Tank Destroyer Bn	20/12/44	1/1/45
591st Field Artillery Bn	20/12/44	11/1/45
740th Tank Bn	29/12/44	11/1/45
	27/1/45	5/2/45
628th Tank Destroyer Bn	1/1/45	11/1/45
517th Parachute Infantry	1/1/45	11/1/45
	1/2/45	4/2/45
634th Anti-Aircraft Artillery Bn	5/2/45	18/2/45
887th Airborne Engineer Coy	25/12/44	12/1/45
Coy A, 87th Chemical Bn	25/1/45	5/2/45
643rd Tank Destroyer Bn	25/1/45	31/1/45
400th Armored Field Artillery Bn	25/1/45	18/2/45
32nd Cavalry Reconnaissance Squadron	28/1/45	5/2/45
629th Tank Destroyer Bn	31/1/45	18/2/45

Central Europe

341st Infantry Regt	4/4/45	4/4/45
417th Field Artillery Group	4/4/45	25/4/45
746th Field Artillery Bn	4/4/45	25/4/45
672nd Field Artillery Bn	4/4/45	14/4/45
541st Field Artillery Bn	4/4/45	25/4/45
805th Field Artillery Bn	4/4/45	6/4/45
546th Field Artillery Bn	11/4/45	16/4/45
790th Field Artillery Bn	10/4/45	14/4/45

74th Cml General Coy	4/4/45	21/4/45
74th Field Artillery Bn	18/4/45	25/4/45
12th Tank Destroyer Group (HQ only)	18/4/45	25/4/45
661st Field Artillery Bn	18/4/45	25/4/45
942d Field Artillery Bn	18/4/45	25/4/45
3rd Coy, 22nd Belgian Fusilier Bn	21/4/45	25/4/45
294th Field Artillery Observation Bn	25/4/45	25/4/45
1130th Engineer C Bn (sic)	25/4/45	26/4/45
280th Field Artillery Bn	27/4/45	17/5/45
580th AAA AW Bn	26/4/45	2/5/45
	23/5/45	5/5/45
13th Infantry	28/4/45	1/5/45
43rd Field Artillery Bn	28/4/45	1/5/45
604th Tank Destroyer Bn	28/4/45	15/5/45
A Squadron, 4th Royals (BR) (sic)	29/4/45	2/5/45
740th Tank Bn	29/4/45	1/5/45
644th Tank Destroyer Bn	29/4/45	1/5/45
Coy A, 89th Chemical Bn	29/4/45	9/5/45
121st Infantry Regt	30/4/45	1/5/45
56th Field Artillery Bn	30/4/45	1/5/45
Coy C, 89th Chemical Bn	30/4/45	1/5/45
CC 'B', 7th Armored Division	1/5/45	4/5/45
205th Field Artillery Group	3/5/45	17/5/45
207th Field Artillery Bn	3/5/45	17/5/45
768th Field Artillery Bn	3/5/45	17/5/45

Military Intelligence Teams (attached in ETO USA}

82nd Counter Intelligence Corps Det
Interrogator Prisoner of War Team No 40
Interrogator Prisoner of War Team No 43
Interrogator Prisoner of War Team No 45
Interrogator Prisoner of War Team No 47
Military Intelligence Interpreter Team No 412
Order of Battle Team No 16
Photo Interpretation Team No 3
Photo Interpretation Team No 11

Above: Wartime units that served as part of or attached to 82nd Airborne Division. Taken from a immediate postwar summary published by the US Army with some missing dates, and some strange unit identifications highlighted (sic) by the editor.

Left: American and British troops rest on the east side of the Elbe after crossing on 30 April 1945. The US troops are of Company I, 505th PIR. (via Real War Photos)

IN ACTION

NORTH AFRICA

After eight months of intensive training at Bragg the 82nd was anxious to get on with the war. The troopers were at a high state of readiness and the war situation was beginning to turn in Africa at least. American paras in the shape of the 509th had been in action during Operation Torch, but the first full-scale use of the Airborne was yet to be undertaken.

In April 1943 orders finally came for deployment overseas to a yet unspecified destination. On the 20th the division began moving by train to Camp Edwards, Massachusetts. This was completed in an air of secrecy, which required the troopers to remove all Airborne insignia and their beloved jump-boots, that they might pass for 'legs' during the transit. Eventually boarding troopships at New York on the 27th the division sailed for North Africa on the 29th.

Conditions on the troopships were less than luxurious but the troopers did their best to cope and keep fit on the long voyage east. Finally, on 10 May the convoy docked at Casablanca. Whilst the ships were unloaded a few days were spent at Camp Don B Passage, before moving out north-eastwards to bivouac camps at Oujda (for the paratroops) and Marnia (for the glider forces).

Here they were joined by the men of the 509th who, with three combat jumps to their credit, naturally felt somewhat superior to the 'green' 82nd. The veterans soon found the newly arrived troopers keen to learn from their experience, however, and the next few weeks of intensive training proceeded apace.

In view of the intense daytime heat, which limited the performance of both men and machines, much of this training was carried out at night. The experience proved invaluable, with the men learning how to group and carry out assaults under a variety of circumstances. The gliders, too, were rehearsed, with much time being devoted to the speedy removal and bringing into action of the heavy equipment they carried.

There was little scope for diversion during this period, although the division attracted its fair share of high-ranking visitors, anxious to see how the new force was shaping up. Visiting 'brass' included their erstwhile commander Omar Bradley, and George Patton who immediately recognised kindred spirits in the tough troopers.

With little outlet for off-duty enthusiasm the troopers turned their energies to occasionally bizarre enterprises. It was for instance considered by some that they needed an animal mascot to replace Max the dog, left behind in the States. This took the form of an unfortunate beast—variously reported as a mule or a jackass—which they tried to train to jump with them. Getting it into a parachute and out of the aircraft was apparently accomplished without problems. Sadly it failed to appreciate the finer points of landing, breaking a leg on its first jump, its consequent demise seemingly a poor reward for considerable equine bravery.

On 24 May Colonel Gavin, one of the regimental commanders, was called to Ridgway's HQ to be briefed on the forthcoming assault on Sicily, Operation Husky, slated for 9 July. Characteristically, Gavin shortly arranged to recce the drop zones (DZs) in person. Gavin, two battalion commanders and two pilots from the 52nd Troop Carrier Wing, took a pair of the unarmed, but very fast British Mosquito aircraft over Sicily. This risky undertaking was fortunately accomplished without loss, and Gavin returned confident that the operation was feasible.

As an aside, the loss, or worse the capture, of such a senior officer would have seriously compromised the operation. Much effort had been expended on disinformation (including the 'Man Who Never Was' operation which allowed the Germans to 'find' a body carrying 'secret' documents indicating an invasion somewhere else). This need to keep the target secret had unfortunate consequences. The troopers were not informed of the presence on Sicily of a Panzer division, lest the fact that they knew that gave away the objective. They were thus insufficiently prepared for the Tiger tanks of the *Hermann Göring* Division they encountered. On 16 June, after six weeks of intensive training, the division moved to Kairouan in Tunisia. The invasion of Europe was about to begin.

OPERATION HUSKY

The Allies, having finally turned the tide of war in North Africa, saw Sicily as a literal stepping-stone into what Churchill described, with typical floridity, as 'the soft underbelly of the Axis'. As earlier related, the Pyrrhic German victory on Crete had spurred the development of airborne forces on both sides of the Atlantic. Roosevelt and Churchill had both taken a personal interest in the development of parachute forces as they could see the potential they offered. It had been decided that resources would be pooled for airborne operations and Sicily was therefore to be the first major test of the whole concept.

As it turned out Sicily was to be an almost unique engagement, British, American and German paratroopers were to meet in combat and many individual acts of heroism were carried out on both sides. As would be expected fighting was tough with little quarter given. The All Americans may have lacked the combat experience of the British and Germans, but their aggressive training ultimately proved more than equal to the task, and probably decisive.

Above: One of a series (see colour section) of photographs taken in North Africa before Operation Husky. This shows well the 1943 equipment. (82nd Airborne Museum)

Sicily was also to provide a salutary lesson in how not to organise a combined-arms assault, and was very nearly an unmitigated disaster. The plan was essentially sound; the execution, however, was another matter.

The problems began with a fairly fundamental dispute between the British and American commanders over who should get what share of the limited number of aircraft assets available. Eventually the British got the bulk of the gliders—and even then had to leave a battalion behind in order to lift all their heavy equipment. The 82nd Regimental Combat Team (RCT) on the other hand would be parachute only.

Whilst the brass were thrashing out the details the troopers were training hard. Although they had not been told of their objective (and would not be until almost the last moment) a training area had been laid out in the desert to simulate the sixteen or so pill boxes surrounding the Gela drop area. These were assaulted with live ammunition until the men were thoroughly rehearsed. As ever the rumour factory was at full production with suggested targets running through most of southern Europe, and at least one that they were to jump on Berlin in order to capture Hitler!

The plan essentially was for the airborne forces to assault key bridges and defensive positions immediately ahead of amphibious landings on the south and east coasts. This, it was hoped, would allow an early breakout from the beachheads and a rapid drive to secure the island.

The British were to go in first in order to secure three key bridges on the east coast road. Shortly behind them the Americans would jump into an area around Gela on the south coast. The British Eighth, and American Seventh Armies respectively would simultaneously follow with sea-borne landings in the same sectors. The first phase airborne landings would go in on the night of D-1/D and be codenamed Husky One (American) and Fustian (British). Support would also be provided in the form of naval gunfire, a provision which very nearly proved to be the undoing of the whole enterprise.

As H-Hour approached the troops bivouacked around Kairouan began assembling at the ten satellite airfields it served. First off were the British at 19.00hrs. They had a motley fleet of 128 Waco CG-4 gliders (provided by the Americans and therefore new to the British pilots) and eight Horsas. Towing aircraft included 109 Dakotas, 21 Albemarles and eight Halifaxes.

A little over an hour later the American lift, some 3,400 soldiers of the 505th and 504th, plus some support elements, also took off. A total of 266 Dakotas formed into flights of nine and headed out over the Mediterranean. Each man had with him a slip of paper with a message from Gavin. 'Slim Jim' did not go in for the grandiloquence of some of his contemporaries, but the inspiration was clear and effective.

Right: The 82nd trained at Oujda and left for Sicily from Kairouan, the aircraft being routed via Malta. During the invasion of Italy, the division saw action at Salerno, and in January 1944 at Anzio. Leaving the theatre in April 1943, the 509th would return in August 1944 to participate in the invasion of southern France.

'Soldiers of the 505th Combat Team.

'Tonight you embark on a combat mission for which our people and the free people of the world have been waiting for two years.

'You will spearhead the landing of an American Force on the island of SICILY. Every preparation has been made to eliminate the element of chance. You have been given the means to do the job and you are backed by the largest assemblage of air power in the world's history.

'The eyes of the world are upon you. The hopes and prayers of every American go with you.

James M. Gavin'

Both lifts were routed via Malta at low level to avoid detection until the last moment. Only as they crossed the coast of Sicily would they gain height to approach the drop zones. Unfortunately visibility was poor, and winds were exceptionally high. Worse, as they flew directly over the naval elements near the beaches the nervous, inexperienced (and unbriefed) gunners below fired upon the lumbering transports of the British lift, believing them to be German bombers. Already dispersed and in some confusion, nearly half the gliders came down in the sea. The paratroops fared little better being dropped far and wide, only one group actually making its allocated DZ. Because of the high winds drop injuries were high, too.

In their turn the Americans also found themselves over Sicily with only the broadest notion as to exactly which part. As was to become typical, Gavin was the first man to jump. not far behind him was 'Red' Ryder, who had commanded the Test Platoon and was now a lieutenant colonel. Also jumping with the 82nd that night was war correspondent Jack Thompson of the *Chicago Tribune*. If anything the 82nd was even more widely dispersed than the British, being spread over some 60km in small groups.

At this point, with the plan in tatters, it might be thought that disaster was inevitable. Although the troopers did not know it yet, fate had actually placed the paras well. For the time being, however, the 82nd's initiative and training in small unit actions took over, and the results were remarkable.

Because of the scattered drop, the German and Italian defenders were faced with ambush and assault by groups of the tough Americans seemingly coming out of the night from all directions. The troopers cut communications, destroyed bunkers and vehicles and generally created havoc in the enemy rear. In some sectors they linked up with the British after an understandable exchange of fire in at least one spot.

Numerous small actions were fought that night. Landing almost amongst the enemy at Ponte Dirillo, G Company, 505th set about clearing the Germans from their trenches and pillboxes, quickly seizing a bridge that would assist the US 45th Infantry Division in its breakout for the beach. Elsewhere 14 paratroops took on a group of pillboxes which they knocked out, capturing some 250 Italians.

Jack Thompson described another such engagement:

'One group of the 1st Battalion, including Lt Colonel Arthur Gorham, landed four miles south of Niscemi, about 2½ miles from the scheduled DZ. They were just east of a very sturdy, thick-walled farmhouse which had been converted into a military fort held by 60 men with 4 heavy machine guns and 6 lights. It was well wired in with trench defences. Colonel Gorham ordered an assault on the house, and it was organised and led by Captain Edwin Sayre and 22 men.

'Their first attack was launched at 2 o'clock in the morning. They were held up then, but attacked again just before dawn, with rifles, grenades, one 60mm mortar and a bazooka. They forced the Italians back out of the trenches and into the house and attacked the house with grenades. Sayre led the assault, carrying one hand grenade in his teeth and another in his left hand, with his carbine in his right hand. It was after they had taken the farmhouse that he discovered that the man who was covering him was armed only with a trench knife and not a tommy gun as he had thought. A rifle grenade fired at about ten feet blew open the door, but the door swung shut again. Sayre walked up, threw open the door, and pitched a hand grenade inside.

'They found a total of 15 dead and took 45 prisoners, some of whom were Germans. Four paratroops were wounded, one of whom later died. The house soon came under fire from an 88, and Col Gorham withdrew his men back to another hill.'

All of this gained time for the beachheads to be consolidated as such action reduced or prevented adequate response from the defending forces. Matters were not all one-sided, however. Unbeknown to most of the troopers, the *Hermann Göring* Panzer Division was on the island, and armed in part at least with the formidable Tiger tank. This division had the potential to throw the invaders back into the sea. The lightly armed paras on the other hand, had only the woefully inadequate bazooka with which to respond. Only marginally effective against medium tanks, its rounds often failed to halt the German behemoth.

Biazza Ridge
Here fate played its hand. Gavin had been separated from most of his command, but by D+1 had managed to link up with around 250 men, mostly from the 3rd Battalion, 505th. Instinctively he headed for high ground overlooking the 45th Infantry's defences in order to drive the Germans off such a commanding position. It was as the Americans pursued the fleeing defenders that they encountered the first Tiger tanks.

The counter-attack was repulsed with some difficulty. A single pack howitzer from the 456th Parachute Field Artillery (PFA) used direct fire, forcing the Germans back at least temporarily. The paras had by chance been dropped between the beach and the Panzers. Keeping the two apart was to prove vital. With the aid of artillery support and naval gunfire Biazza Ridge was held, but at a high cost in casualties amongst the All Americans.

Above: Gavin jumped with his men and led from the front. Here he is 'chuting up for the D-Day jump, note his preferred weapon, a rifle. (82nd Airborne Museum)

Other elements of the *Hermann Göring* Division encountered the tenacious Americans dug-in with two captured Italian anti-tank guns along the Niscemi–Biscari Highway. Here the 3rd Battalion, 504th drove off a German column heading for the beaches. One or two Tigers actually traded fire with off-shore destroyers, but thanks to the courageous efforts of the paras there was to be no armoured attack on the beaches of any consequence.

The plethora of actions underway all over southern Sicily actually led the defenders to believe that they were under attack by 'five or more' airborne divisions. In fact, fewer than 200 paras had seized and held all the objectives assigned to the whole combat team. The massive disruption caused by the rest, however, had ensured that the response by Axis forces to the sea-borne assault was blunted.

Disaster strikes

The plan called for a second wave to jump on Farello airfield on D+1. Despite the lessons of the first drop, and against Ridgway's misgivings, it went ahead as planned, there being no time to re-plan such a complex undertaking. It was to prove the biggest disaster of the 82nd's war.

The drop was to consist of the rest of the 504th, the 376th Parachute Artillery, and the balance of the 307th Parachute Engineer Battalion. Commanding the 2nd Battalion, 504th was Bill Yarborough.

The first C-47s over the DZ dropped their charges without incident, but as the second wave came in, all hell broke loose. It was never established exactly who had fired the first shot, but an AA gunner who fired at the lumbering Dakotas, believing them to be enemy bombers, panicked those around him into opening up. Almost instantly a fire-storm of machine-gun and cannon fire enveloped the hapless transports.

Some 23 out of 144 C-47s were destroyed, and dozens of others were terribly shot-up. Worse, the AA batteries continued to fire on the paras that did jump, and on aircraft that had managed to ditch in the sea. More than 300 aircrew and paras were killed and hundreds more badly injured. Less than 25% of the lift made it onto the DZ.

This incident almost led to the demise of Airborne units in the post mortem that followed the Sicily operations. As with the German experience in Crete, there were those who felt that the cost could not be justified. Certainly the Marine Corps, which had been considering forming parachute units, quietly shelved its plans in the light of such a predictable disaster—the cause of which was routing friendly transports over surface elements who were inevitably under attack from enemy aircraft.

By this time the Germans had already realised that Sicily was going to fall. This did not mean they were going to give up without a battle and a fighting withdrawal was planned that would make the Allies pay for every yard gained.

For the rest of the Sicilian campaign the 82nd served as infantry with Patton's Seventh Army. In view of the casualties suffered in the initial jumps (and the need to conserve the highly trained paratroops for future use) they were not assigned the hardest missions. This in no way reduced their aggressiveness or resolve and the 82nd continued to lead by example, capturing at one point the vital port of Trapani and some 5,000 prisoners.

By 22 July the Americans were in Palermo, and Sicily effectively fell to the Allies on 14 August. On the 16th, just hours ahead of the British, Patton's men entered Messina. The battle for Sicily was over.

INTO ITALY

With Sicily secure, the Allies were anxious to press on across the Straits of Messina and into Italy proper. They rightly surmised that the Italians were minded to surrender or even change sides following the removal of Mussolini from power.

Hitler, having reached the same estimation of Italian steadfastness, had vastly strengthened his forces on the peninsula, and at one point had Student's *Fallschirmjäger* amongst troops poised to take part in the 'arrest' of the entire Italian government and the Crown Prince. In the light of this somewhat fluid situation Allied planning went through several iterations. At least six plans for airborne assault were considered and discarded.

The Taylor Mission
A plan that very nearly happened saw the 82nd actually 'chuted up' for a drop on Rome, where, with the assistance of Italian forces, they were to seize the city from the Germans. Fortunately for the troopers this dangerous plan was cancelled at the last moment following a remarkable personal meeting between the 82nd's Divisional Artillery Commander Brigadier General Maxwell D. Taylor and Marshal Badoglio, the head of the new Italian government, actually in occupied Rome.

This mission was the stuff of adventure movies, placing a member of the 82nd at a pivotal point in history. It also proves that whilst fighting skills may be fundamental to the success of airborne soldiers, their innate quick thinking and ability to adapt in changing situations is equally important. It also possibly demonstrates that the best officers and soldiers are attracted to élite units, which in turn is why they perform better than 'average' formations.

The Italians were indeed anxious to capitulate, but feared massive German reprisals against Rome the moment the surrender was announced. The plan therefore called for a drop to prevent this, timed to coincide with the sea-borne landing at Salerno. The Italians were to provide security and support which would be essential to the success of the mission. Their actual ability to do this was

Below: General Mark Clark speaks to members of the 325th Glider Infantry near Salerno. The 82nd had been able to stabilise the beachhead at Salerno, and Clark later specifically requested elements of the 82nd remain in Italy after the bulk of the Division returned to the UK. (U.S. Army)

Above: General Mark Clark flanked by British Generals Alexander (left) and McCreery on the beach at Salerno. (US Army via George Forty)

severely doubted and it was decided that a face-to-face meeting was necessary. General Taylor spoke Italian and accompanied by Colonel Tuder Gardiner, left Palermo on 7 September for the clandestine meeting.

Just off Ustica island they transferred to an Italian corvette for the short voyage to the port of Gaeta. The execution of the drop now depended on a radio message from Taylor. On arrival the two Americans 'roughed themselves up' and, masquerading as prisoners, were bundled into a car by their Italian escort. A dangerous trip through hostile territory and German roadblocks eventually brought them to Rome.

Much to Taylor's frustration the ageing Badoglio had to be roused from his bed for the immediate conference that was needed. It soon became apparent that the Italians were in no position to guarantee the support that the 82nd would require. Taylor's first task was to cancel the drop. Coded radio messages were urgently sent and finally at 16.30hrs—as the first troopers were boarding their aircraft—the drop for that evening was cancelled. Had Taylor been captured or killed and not sent the abort message, the 82nd would have dropped into a disaster that night.

Taylor meanwhile found himself the *de facto* Allied negotiator for the Italian armistice. He insisted that Badoglio write a message to Eisenhower confirming that the Italians could not support Operation Giant II (as the Rome drop was code-named) and that he (Taylor) was to return to Sicily to convey the views of the Italian government. The signed, longhand, message now in his hand, Taylor radioed its content and awaited orders.

Having sat through an American air raid, Taylor eventually received orders to return. Together with Deputy Chief of the Italian Defence Staff, General Rossi, the two American soldiers once again embarked on a hair-raising trip past the occupying Germans (at one point a column of infantry passed within yards of the small truck they were trying to be inconspicuous in). Safely reaching an Italian airfield they were flown to Algeria in an Italian SM 79 (with the attendant risk of being shot down by their own forces).

As planned Eisenhower announced the surrender as the first soldiers were hitting the Salerno beaches on the 9th. An hour later Badoglio, despite his fears about German reprisals, confirmed it in a radio broadcast to the Italian people.

Salerno
The Allied invasion of Italy began with landings at Salerno (Operation Avalanche) on the east coast, and simultaneously at Taranto (Operations Gibbon and Slapstick). German resistance at Salerno proved stiff, and the attackers were soon bogged down on the beachheads. Matters reaching a critical point on the afternoon of the 13th when Ridgway, at the time en route by air to a command conference, received a radio message from Lieutenant General Mark Clark, commander of Fifth Army, urgently requesting a drop to stem a threatened Axis breakthrough of Allied lines.

In a remarkable demonstration of their ability to respond the 504th RCT was stepping out over the drop zone to execute an almost text-book landing exactly eight hours later, the soldiers having been briefed in the aircraft as the engines were started. Together with the 325th GIR the troopers quickly established a perimeter in the area of Paestum. The paratroopers had taken on three German divisions.

The following day the position was consolidated when 1,900 more men of the 504th were dropped. Gavin's 505th RCT also dropped on the beachhead on the 14th, whilst the 2nd Battalion, 509th (attached to the 82nd) dropped in the Avellino sector and set about disrupting defences, communications and supplies in the enemy rear.

This latter drop, into mountainous terrain, again suffered from dispersion, with the 640 men dropped spread over nearly 100 square miles. Only 510 eventually made it back to Allied lines, but for nearly three weeks their activities tied down a totally disproportionate number of German troops (more in fact than the number available to the whole Allied command) who were thus unavailable to the action around Salerno.

Whilst the drops were going in, the 325th Glider Infantry, together with 3rd Battalion, 504th were sailing for Salerno from Licata. On arrival on the night of the 15th the 325th moved to begin operations in the Sorrento peninsula, whilst the 504th's men rejoined their regiment at Albanella. The following morning the 504th marched some four miles to occupy the town, and by noon Colonel Tucker was briefing his battalion commanders to seize and hold high ground overlooking Altavilla, key positions that would protect the security of the beachheads.

This was to be no small undertaking. Not only was a greatly superior force ranged against the Americans, but the valley floor they were going to have to cross had for some years been a German artillery range. This meant that hostile fire was very accurate and could concentrate on almost any spot with precision. Most of the American casualties over the next three days were directly attributable to artillery fire.

By the 17th the 504th had nevertheless taken all its objectives. The regiment was, however, now cut off from Allied lines and that night it was suggested by General Dawley, commander of the VI Corps, that the 504th withdraw and try to form a line closer to the beaches. Tucker's famous 'Retreat, Hell!' response resulted in the reinforcements he wanted being sent and the ground was held, enabling the Fifth Army to move northwards towards Salerno and Naples.

The advance continues

Meanwhile F Company, 325th took to boats to occupy the island of Ischia in the Bay of Naples. The remaining elements of the 82nd also arrived by sea at the tiny village of Maiori, which clung to the sheer rock of the mountains above. The aim was to drive the Germans from the heights, and, together with Colonel Darby's Rangers, the 325th RCT and 3rd Battalion, 504th started climbing, successfully clearing the enemy as they went. Mt San Argela and the Chiunzi pass were taken,

Below: Anzio X-Ray beach soon after the landings. (US Army via George Forty)

enabling a link up with H Company, 504th, which was holding out alongside the 319th Battalion Glider Field Artillery and the Rangers. The remainder of the 504th took up positions on the Chiunzi pass on 25 September, and by the following day was overlooking the Naples plain. The pass quickly became known as '88 pass' for the concentration of enemy fire directed on it.

By the 29th the 505th, now attached to the British 23rd Armoured Brigade, was moving towards Naples. The next day elements of the 505th became the first reconnaissance troops in the city. The 504th, with the British XX Corps, meanwhile skirted the base of Mt Vesuvius to bypass the city. When, on 1 October, Naples duly became the first major European city to fall to the Allies, the 82nd was in the vanguard of the victorious troops that marched in.

For most of the 82nd there followed a period of policing duties in Naples. Whilst sporadic German attacks continued, and they had to deal with sabotage attempts and booby traps, the troopers had time for some relaxation finding the bars (and other rather less salubrious establishments) much to their liking after the deserts of North Africa.

The 505th on the other hand, continued north towards the Volturno River with the British, spending the 3rd to the 9th clearing pockets of resistance. Characteristically the 505th was amongst the first across on the 13th.

On 29 October the 504th began an epic drive through the mountains. With the Fifth Army on its left and the Eighth Army on its right the leaders were eventually 22 miles ahead. Crossing the Volturno the paratroops entered Isernia, a major road and rail junction, and cleared Calli, Macchio, Fornelli, Cerro and Rochetta. During the entire period all actions were small unit engagements. There was no defined front line and both sides roamed the area. The men of the 82nd, however, were masters at this type of work, besting the Germans on virtually every occasion. The terrain was extremely difficult and roads were all but non-existent. Everything had to be carried by mule or by man-power. Evacuating casualties meant hours toiling down mountain tracks with stretchers.

Despite all problems it was eventually just 15 troopers who crossed a minefield to take Hill 1017, Fifth Army's primary objective.

In November the bulk of the division was due to move to Ireland to begin training for the forthcoming invasion of France. At the specific request of Mark Clark, however, the 504th along with the 376th Field Artillery Battalion and elements of the 307th Airborne Engineers remained in Italy with his Fifth Army. The rest of the 82nd sailed on the 18th. Between 10 and 27 December the 504th was in combat in the Venafro sector, participating in the seizure of Mt Summairo.

ANZIO

On 21/22 January Fifth Army's assault on Anzio (Operation Shingle) commenced, the 504th landing near Nettuno. The landing at first proceeded like a training exercise, but as the leading LCTs were unloading, the Luftwaffe arrived. Despite ferocious AA fire from the ships the attacking aircraft wrought terrible destruction on the beachhead. Under repeated attack the men and equipment mostly got ashore, but considerable losses were sustained. After some two days the regiment was ordered to the right flank of the beachhead, taking up positions along the Mussolini canal.

Over the next few days the Allies attempted to break out, the 504th capturing several bridges after bruising firefights with a heavily armed enemy. Attacks on the

25th by all three battalions pushed towards Borgo Piave, an important road junction. Whilst the attacks were successful initially, the Germans countered with an armoured force which eventually pushed the 504th back to the canal.

This situation continued for several days, until the 504th was relieved by the 179th Infantry. After a short respite in reserve the 3rd Battalion, now attached to the 1st Armored Division, was committed with the British 1st Division in the Carroceto sector.

There the battalion suffered many casualties to unprecedented enemy artillery fire, and when German infantry finally attacked it was only the tough troopers' iron-will and steadiness under fire that enabled them to repel repeated assaults. Accounts of the often hand-to-hand fighting are harrowing and it is clear that lesser troops would have buckled.

The fighting between 8 and 12 February was savage. At one stage H Company was able to recapture a senior British officer from the Germans, and with the assistance of I Company fight its way back to the Allied lines. Such actions earned the 3rd Battalion one of the first Presidential Unit Citations awarded in the European theatre.

The battle for Anzio quickly became a static defensive, matter of attrition—not what airborne troops are trained for, and a waste of their skills. It was with considerable relief therefore that the men of the 504th finally received orders for England on 25 March. They left Anzio for Naples in LSTs, still under fire, and finally arrived in England on 10 April. The 82nd's war in Italy had finished. The troopers had more than proved themselves in combat but suffered terrible casualties in the process. Ahead of them was an even bigger task.

Below: The landings at Anzio were heavily contested. The 82nd came in by sea, the 504th PIR landing under attack from the Luftwaffe. (US Army via George Forty)

THE INVASION OF NORMANDY

In November 1943, as the bulk of the 82nd prepared to leave the Mediterranean, General Gavin had already gone to London to help plan the airborne part of the forthcoming invasion of France. The soldiers, after months in warm climes, were shortly to find themselves in Northern Ireland in winter. There might not be anyone shooting at them there, but the change from southern to northern European weather was certainly going to test their hardiness. The 82nd had suffered terrible casualties and was going to need some time to get back to full strength. It had also proved beyond doubt the value of the Airborne and that meant the call would not be long in coming.

The division was not to stay in Ireland for long. Early in the New Year a more permanent facility was set up near Leicester. To make up strength the 507th and 508th PIRs were now assigned to the division. Additionally volunteers were sought amongst suitably qualified replacement troops arriving from the US—in most cases only too happy to leave the miserable tented camps in the dank Welsh countryside they were 'holding' in. A jump school was established near Leicester to qualify those not previously parachute trained, and training at all levels was stepped up.

The nine months spent in England were generally happy ones for the troopers. They found that they had much in common with their British counterparts and, of course, there was a social life. The locals were for the most part welcoming and friendly, the girls pretty and the beer, if unfamiliar to American tastes, was good. Again from the modern perspective, it should be remembered that many of the troopers had known nothing of the world outside a farm in Nebraska or Tennessee a few months before.

Another important step came in England. The glidermen, long denied parity with the paratroops they so ably supported, finally received their pay increase and their own wings. No one truly begrudged it—jumping was always regarded as far safer than going by glider.

As the intensive training continued, so did the build-up of men and material for the invasion. Over 2,000 Waco gliders were shipped to the UK and assembled. In order that the 101st should benefit from the combat experience of the 82nd Gavin was put in charge of standardising tactics and procedures throughout the Airborne.

The British Isles became a vast hive of military activity as every arm of service from dozens of nations prepared for the biggest invasion in history. The Reich was pounded by the RAF at night and by the US Army Air Force during the day. Every possible logistic need was considered, huge floating harbours and fuel pipelines were devised; new equipment was developed and tested and assaults from the sea and air rehearsed. Occasionally the exercises were all too real. Terrible slaughter was wrought off the Dorset coast one night when German E-Boats got in amongst landing craft full of troops. (Kept secret at the time lest it effected morale, the disaster at Slapton Sands has only recently been fully reported.)

There were problems at the top, too. For all the public unity amongst the Allies there were disagreements and conflicting agendas, both political and military. Later on this was to cost the Airborne dear. For the time being a consensus was eventually reached, and planning for Operation Overlord went into the final stages. Gavin rejoined the division on 6 February.

D-Day plans

There were a number of possibilities considered, including the extremes of an airborne assault on Paris (which would be held until a link up with the sea-borne invasion force) and dropping the troops directly on the coastal defences at the

Above right: Waco CG-4 (Hadrians to the British) gliders in invasion stripes landing in Normandy, June 1944. the stripes were put on the wings in great secrecy a few days before the invasion. (82nd Airborne Museum)

Below right: Build-up to D-Day: assembling CG-4 gliders out of packing cases somewhere in England, 1944. (82nd Airborne Museum)

Above: Gavin briefing officers for a jump. The photo was taken in England prior to D-Day—the carefully posed group appear to be in a British Nissen hut, prefabricated building built largely from corrugated iron sheets. These were universal on UK bases and many survive to this day (82nd Airborne Museum)

beaches. More sanguine heads prevailed and eventually it was decided that the first Allied soldiers on French soil were indeed to be paratroops dropping ahead of the sea-borne landing. They would, however, drop inland to serve as a blocking force preventing reinforcements reaching the invasion beaches, and simultaneously seizing vital roads and bridges that would enable a breakout from the beachhead in due course. As ever they would also create as much confusion and havoc as possible in the enemy rear.

The US airborne troops were to arrive in Normandy in three different ways. Some 18,000 men from the 82nd and 101st would drop by parachute. Close behind them would be the gliders, and finally a small contingent (principally artillery) would come in across Utah Beach.

The final plan—its last revision made only a few days before the invasion—called for the 82nd to drop on both sides of the Merderet River in order to secure Neuville-au-Plain, Ste-Mère-Église, Chef-du-Pont, Etienville, Amfreville and their surrounding areas. They were also to destroy bridges across the Douve River denying German reinforcements that route to the beaches.

To provide some measure of mutual support should things go badly on the beaches, the 101st's DZs were close to those of the 82nd. Some re-assignment of objectives saw the 82nd draw Ste-Mère-Église originally slated for the 101st. This irony was reversed a few months later when the 101st got the toughest assignment at Bastogne by equal happenstance.

The gliders were to undertake the first operational night landing ever attempted hopefully with the aid of beacons set up by pathfinders dropped ahead of them. There were not going to be enough gliders or pilots so some of the glider infantry and artillery were going to have to be part of the amphibious landing and link up with the rest of the division as soon as possible.

Originally D-Day was to be 5 June, but bad weather forced a postponement. Troopers by this time were already at the airfields and ports. The 456th PFA for instance had boarded ship at Rothgate dock in Cardiff on 3 June, its vehicles and guns having been loaded over the previous few days. Airfields all over southern England were lined with aircraft bearing the hastily applied black and white 'invasion stripes' mandated for the day. (Aircraft recognition was poor throughout armies in 1944, and the Allies wanted no repeat of the Sicily debacle.)

At 17.15hrs on the 5th the 456th was amongst a growing armada that set sail for France, at about the same time as the paratroopers were checking their equipment and weapons. They expected to be on their own for a while before the 'legs' got off the beaches and were consequently heavily armed in addition to their bulky T5 parachutes and reserves. Troopers carried as much ammunition, grenades and fighting knives as could physically be managed. Most men hefted nearly 100 pounds of equipment—making the mandatory yellow 'Mae West' life preserver a somewhat doubtful assistance in the event of a water landing. Surprisingly few accidents were reported in the circumstances, although the 505th suffered three killed and ten wounded when a grenade exploded as its men were boarding their aircraft.

At around 23.00hrs the first pathfinders took off, and a little over an hour later over 1,000 C-47s were following them. The greatest invasion in history was under way. Some 378 of these aircraft carried the 82nd's three regiments with 52 gliders accompanying them with anti-tank guns and other heavy equipment.

The assault force was to fly what today would be called a 'lo-hi-lo' profile. Crossing the English Channel at 500 feet or less to avoid radar, they would climb

Below: Soldiers of the 508th PIR checking their T-5 parachutes on an airfield in England prior to D-Day. Note the variety of fighting knives and pistols, as well as the cargo pockets bulging with extra ammunition or supplies. None of the soldiers has yet donned his reserve 'chute, so the harness detail can be seen. (US Army)

to 1,500 feet while crossing the coast in an attempt to escape German small-arms fire and light flak, before dropping once again to 500 feet as they approached the drop zones.

D-Day

The first pathfinders were on French soil at 01.21hrs on 6 June. Unfortunately many were off course and consequently did not turn on their beacons. First aircraft over the DZs were carrying the 101st who managed a reasonably accurate drop. Unfortunately for the following 82nd this meant that the defences were now thoroughly alerted. Heavy flak forced many aircraft off course and Gavin's men were widely scattered. The gliders, too, had eventful flights. Broken tows and other problems forced some back. One CG-4 had the hinged nose section unlatch in flight, and since this contained the pilots, a fairly hairy few minutes were had whilst frantic attempts were made to secure it. With considerable difficulty this section made it back to base.

Meanwhile the paratroopers were discovering that aerial reconnaissance had failed to reveal marshy ground—at best this slowed them down, and at worst literally swallowed some of their heavy equipment. Some troopers came down in rivers. Only the 505th was dropped near its planned drop zone. Men of the 3rd/505th under Lt Colonel Krause headed for their objective, Ste-Mère-Église. To their horror they found the bodies of troopers who had fallen directly on the town in the drop and had been killed by the Germans before they could assemble their weapons and defend themselves.

Before dawn—less than four hours after the drop—Ste-Mère-Église became the first town in France to be liberated, at 04.30hrs Krause's men raised the same Stars and Stripes that had flown over Naples when it too was liberated. (Today the same, somewhat battered, flag is proudly displayed in the 82nd Division's museum at Fort Bragg.) The men had precious little time to savour the moment, for at 09.30hrs the Germans counter-attacked, supported by tanks. With some time yet to pass before they could be reinforced from Utah Beach, the troopers of the 82nd were going to have to tough it out.

The 2nd/505th was diverted from its advance on Neuville-au-Plain to reinforce its colleagues. The CO, Lt Colonel Vandervoort, detached a reinforced rifle platoon, together with one of the few 57mm anti-tank guns to survive the landings, with orders to block German attempts to reach the town. This decision proved vital in the coming hours. For four hours the 48 men under Lieutenant Turner Turnbull held off a far superior German force, but suffered some 20% casualties. Together with the defence of Ste-Mère-Église itself the 82nd's heroic stand that morning blunted the German counter-attack on the beaches. Later that evening glidermen from the 325th reinforced the hard-pressed paras.

The 1st/505th meanwhile was attempting to take the bridge over the Merderet River at La Fière. Three assaults, however, had failed with heavy casualties. Gavin, dropped some three miles away, had managed to gather some 500 troopers and sent half of them to assist at La Fière, whilst the rest were ordered to take the Chef-du-Pont bridge, which also crossed the Merderet River. Both bridges were served by narrow causeways across the surrounding boggy ground and were vital if the Utah infantry were to get off the beaches. The problem with this strategy was that bridges work both ways, so keeping them open also meant that the enemy had access to the beaches if they were not held.

The village was taken, as was the eastern end of the bridge, hours later. However the attackers had not managed to gain the other side, and were considering

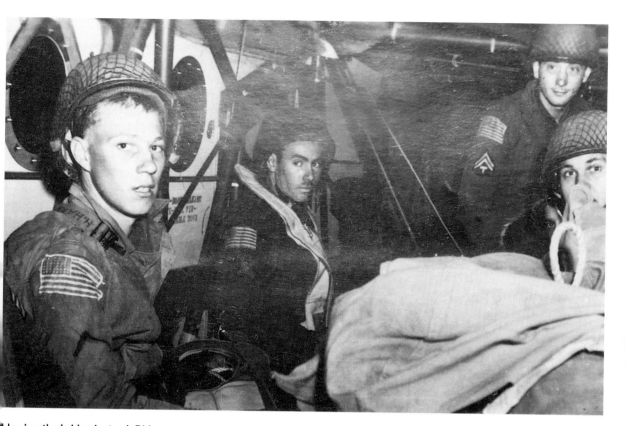

Above: They look too young to go to war—82nd glidermen in a CG-4 over England in 1944. On the night of 5/6 June these men would land on the Cotentin Peninsula. (82nd Airborne Museum)

blowing the bridge instead. Ridgway meanwhile ordered Gavin to take and hold the La Fière causeway and bridge 'at all costs' and efforts were re-doubled. Eventually a company from the 507th (who had suffered bad scattering, some troopers landing 20 miles away) forced its way across the bridge, clearing the Germans from the other side. Inexplicably they then kept going, leaving a vacuum quickly exploited by the Germans who held the western side for a further two days. Despite this, and again with the aid of one of the few 57mm guns available, the 82nd made sure that the Germans could not advance either, knocking out a tank actually on the bridge and interdicting the eastern causeway.

Like the 507th, the 508th had been badly scattered, getting only seven sticks into the regimental DZ. Many of its members found themselves fighting alongside the Screaming Eagles of the 101st (proving the wisdom of standardising tactics) whilst the rest, as in Sicily, fought numerous small actions wherever they could stir up the most chaos. Once again this caused great confusion amongst the Germans who assumed that they were under attack by a far greater force, and were unable to pinpoint the best counter-attack. One group ambushed a staff car and killed General Wilhelm Falley, commander of the German 91st Infantry Division, a major blow to the German command structure.

Elsewhere, the CO of the 2nd/508th, Lt Colonel Thomas J.B. Shanley, rounded up enough troopers to try for his original objective, a bridge over the Douve River. Meeting more resistance than his small force could overcome he withdrew to 'Hill 30' which they then held for two days against numerous counter-attacks. Since this position interdicted the German advance on Chef-du-Pont and thus Ste-Mère-Eglise it became key to the 82nd Division's entire area. Again the ability of airborne soldiers to adapt to a changing tactical situation quickly and decisively had proved its value.

Above: Dated 4 June 1944, this photograph of a group of 'Glider Riders' (probably the 325th) have been hanging around for some time waiting for the order to go (the drop was eventually postponed for 24 hours). Note the chap 'aiming' his bazooka at someone off camera. The two troopers to his left are carrying containers of ammunition for the bazooka. The Horsa they are about to board speaks of hasty reassignment—it displays very roughly applied invasion stripes and someone has marked out, but not had time to finish painting, a US 'star 'n' bar' cockade over the British roundel. The blue part of the insignia has been applied, probably sprayed with a stencil, but only a couple of brush strokes of white. (82nd Airborne Museum)

Left: 509th drop into Southern France, August 1944. (via Bruce Robertson)

Opposite page, Above: Horsa gliders loading for D-Day in England. Once the decision to go was made the troops were confined to barracks and the aircraft painted with the distinctive black and white 'invasion stripes' shown here. Two of the three troopers in the foreground wear (rather loosely) the yellow Mae West life jacket issued for over water flights. The men under the glider wing on the left of the picture are checking the attachment point for the towing yoke. All the gliders visible in the original print have the yoke fitted and are ready to go. (82nd Airborne Museum)

Opposite page, Below: Hamilcar glider in Normandy seen with a DD (swimmable) Sherman.

Right: The airborne landings and the German reaction. The landings on both flanks of the invasion beaches succeeded in drawing away from the beaches German reserves that would otherwise have been used on the 6th. Initially, 21st Panzer was directed at the British on the eastern side of the Orne, while the American units were counter-attacked by 91st and 352nd Divisions. (Map info from Kershaw: *D-Day: Piercing the Atlantic Wall*)

Below: The 82nd and 101st landings were considerably widespread—some 25 miles long by 15 deep. On the morning of the 6th, the 82nd could muster only 33% of its strength, the 101st only 38%. However, this did have the advantage of giving German counter-attackers the problem of where to focus their attacks. (Map info from Kershaw: *D-Day: Piercing the Atlantic Wall*)

The situation changed so quickly because of the imprecise nature of airborne arrival. The paratroopers suffered scattering for a number of reasons: navigational errors were common; anti-aircraft fire could force the aircraft to take evasive action; wind speeds and directions might differ from those estimated. Furthermore in the time it took a stick of troops to exit the C-47's single door the aircraft would travel nearly a mile. Finally wartime T5 and T7 parachutes were designed simply to get the wearer to the ground. They were not the sophisticated 'flyable' canopies that can be deployed today (albeit that they were vastly better than their German WWII equivalents which were not steerable at all).

During the chaotic first few hours of the invasion some troopers literally fell into the hands of the Germans and were captured. One such was 3rd/508th's Battalion Surgeon, Captain Briand N. Boaudin. Released by his comrades a few days later near Orglandes he commandeered, amongst other souvenirs, a rather fine German medical kit which survives at Fort Bragg to this day.

The 'glider riders' faced many of the same problems, including of course, the fact that once free of their tug aircraft they were committed to land in short order no matter what. In Normandy the first night glider landings ever were undertaken, multiplying the dangers. During the two phases (the bulk of the glider force was scheduled for the evening of D-Day) some 11% casualties were suffered just in landing, and only one in four gliders landed undamaged.

Where LZs were blocked, mined or flooded the pilots had to find the nearest open space and try to get in, hedgerows and other obstacles, natural or man-made, notwithstanding. In the confined spaces available many landings were little more than controlled crashes. A final hazard was the load itself. Several aircraft were found with their crews crushed by loads that had torn loose in the landing. Generally, however, the smaller American CG-4s, with their welded tube construction, proved more survivable in Normandy than the bigger, heavier British Horsas. Their wooden construction splintered in a bad landing, giving rise to even more potential for injury amongst the unfortunate occupants.

Above: Liberated Ste-Mère-Église, 6 June 1944. (via Real War Photos)

Below: This picture has often been miscaptioned. It actually shows two 82nd infantrymen, Capt Briand N. Boaudin (left) and Lt Paul E. Lehman. They were captured on D-Day but liberated a few days later. In the process the pair have acquired a number of souvenirs (the French Wine was also liberated from the Germans). Boaudin, a medical officer, holds the German medical valise, with its distinctive cowhide cover, now in the Divisional Museum. (US Army)

Above: Paratroopers move cautiously through a French village in Normandy in June 1944. (US Army via Chris Ellis)

Left: Unidentified Paratroopers move through Carentan in the Cherbourg peninsula. Heavy fighting had secured the town but resulted in considerable damage as can be seen. (US Army via Chris Ellis)

Right and Inset: Lt Kelso C. Horne on the road to St. Sauveur, Normandy in late June 1944. Festooned with bandoliers of extra .30 ammunition for his M1 Garand rifle, Horne also has a grenade clipped to his webbing and a .45 automatic in a leather holster. Although not terribly accurate the .45 was a powerful weapon at close quarters and was reputed to be able to stop a truck. One of the sequence of photos taken at this time later became famous on the cover of *Life* magazine. (US Army via Chris Ellis)

Presidential Unit Citation for HQ and HQ Company, 82nd Airborne cited in War Department General Orders 69 of 22 August 1944

Division HQ and HQ Company, 82nd Airborne Division, is cited for outstanding performance of duty in action against the enemy between 6 and 9 June 1944 during the invasion of France. The Forward Echelon of Division HQ and HQ Company landed by parachute and glider on D-day . . . on the Cotentin Peninsula in the area surrounding Ste-Mère-Église, France. The enemy opposed drops and landings with intense antiaircraft fire and immediately surrounded the secured area with mobile antiairborne landing groups which attacked with machine guns, mortars, and artillery. Shortly after 0200, a division command post was established west of Ste-Mère-Église. HQ personnel were augmented by predawn glider elements landing about 0410, and by further gliderborne increments during the day. HQ personnel from many gliders, which had landed in areas not secured by parachute troops, fought their way to the Division Command Post, into which they infiltrated during the first 48 hours. The Division Staff and HQ Company remained in close proximity to the forward lines at all times. During the first 37 hours, enemy action was often not more than a few hundred yards from the command post. The officers and men of Division HQ and HQ Company labored without rest or relaxation day and night during the first 3 days of the invasion, at times under direct attack by artillery and small-arms, immediately adjacent to active fighting and frequently subjected to bombing attacks directed against it nearby artillery batters. Duties were performed unhesitatingly with utter disregard for personal safety and with superior efficiency and tireless devotion to duty. The courage and perseverance shown by members of the Division HQ and HQ Company, 82nd Airborne Division, are worthy of emulation and reflect the highest traditions of the Army of the United States.

The second landings should have been easier with the advantage of daylight. Unfortunately not only were the planned LZs still contested, but Ridgway's radios had dropped in the river and he thus had no way of warning the incoming gliders that new sites had been hastily marked out.

Again fate played a hand. Still unaware of the situation on the ground the gliders actually arrived an hour early at around 20.00hrs. In this case the almost inevitable navigational errors led to many gliders being off course and actually missing the worst fire from an enemy massed around their intended LZ. The following morning, when the last of the 325th's glidermen arrived, they too suffered from the difficult terrain, losing nearly 200 killed or injured during the landings.

Joining up with elements of the 4th Infantry Division, tanks and their own infantry driving up from the beach, the 325th fought its way towards Ridgway's positions. There the La Fière Bridge was still in German hands and one battalion was sent to help the hard-pressed paratroopers fighting for its control.

By the 8th the 82nd was in control of most of its area of operation, but still the bridge held out. During the day, however, Ridgway learned of a submerged crossing over the Merderet which would enable him to flank the Germans and at 23.00hrs the 1st/325th began the assault.

The fighting was fierce. During this action one platoon became cut off and was threatened with annihilation. As the Germans moved in for what they assumed would be an easy kill Pfc Charles N. de Glopper, already wounded, left cover blazing away with his Browning Automatic Rifle (BAR). He was eventually cut down by return fire but his sacrifice allowed the rest of his platoon to escape. He was posthumously awarded the division's first Medal of Honor in WWII.

It was to take a further assault led by the 3rd/325th, supported with tanks and artillery, before the bridge was finally cleared the following morning. Gavin immediately led a drive to relieve Shanley's men, still holding out on Hill 30. Even at this late stage where operations in the airhead were regarded as 'mopping up' another German counter-attack against La Fière had to be fought off before the area could truly be considered secure.

As the beachheads were consolidated the 82nd found its men being used as assault troops. Driving across the Douve on 14 June they cleared the enemy from some 100 square miles of territory in less than 48 hours. By the 16th they were in control of St Sauveur-le-Vicomte, allowing the 9th Division to pass through their lines and reach the coast on the following day in preparation for the drive on Cherbourg.

During the ensuing days the division turned south and took dozens of objectives against tenacious German resistance to consolidate the bridgehead. Often they were days ahead of the 'legs' divisions designated for the objectives who were moving much more slowly.

After 33 days of constant combat the 82nd was withdrawn from the front line having suffered almost 50% casualties. It had undoubtedly been pivotal in preventing the Germans pushing the allies back into the sea. The Airborne had once again demonstrated its value, but at terrible cost. Captain Charles W. Mason wrote a succinct summary:

'33 days of action without relief, without replacements. Every mission accomplished. No ground gained ever relinquished.'

A better tribute to those who died would be hard to find.

NIJMEGEN

Above: The target—Nijmegen bridge, captured by 82nd Division after savage fighting. (via Bruce Robertson)

During 33 days of fighting in Normandy the division had suffered the highest casualties of any of its campaigns, 46%. This sacrifice, however, certainly prevented far greater slaughter on the beaches. The 82nd's aggression and skill at arms was self-evident. During that time it took on five German divisions, virtually eliminating two of them as effective forces. In this process it destroyed 62 tanks and 44 assorted artillery pieces, plus other materiel too numerous to list. With a record like this it was always going to be at the sharp end—indeed high casualties were expected and allowed for in the macabre calculations of war.

Returning to its bases in England the 82nd set about re-building. Replacements had to be trained, lessons learnt put into practice, equipment replaced and weary troopers given some respite. Whilst the 82nd was recovering the war went on. The division's old friends the 509th had become part of the 1st Airborne Task Force which launched Operation Dragoon, the assault on the French Mediterranean coast, on 15 August. During this operation 90% of the gliders involved were wrecked beyond recovery—but the objectives were taken in less than half the time planned, another vindication of the Airborne.

There was slow progress in the Normandy battles into July but the breakout into northern France then got going with remarkable speed, Paris was liberated on 25 August, and the Allies were rolling back German forces so fast that they were in danger of outrunning supplies. Amidst all this success, however, there were cracks in the alliance that threatened the whole process.

At the highest level the Free French leader General de Gaulle was barely speaking to Roosevelt and on less than friendly terms with Churchill. At the next level down things were little better amongst the military commanders. Many were already thinking about their post-war careers and acting accordingly. Supreme Commander Eisenhower found himself embroiled in conflicting proposals from rival commanders. On the one hand there was the autocratic Montgomery who, despite his success in the Western Desert, had a reputation for slow and ponderous manoeuvre. On the other were the redoubtable Omar Bradley (original commander of the re-activated 82nd Infantry Division) and his subordinate George Patton for whom the word 'aggressive' might have been invented. With political considerations and personal vanity also factors it is little wonder that relations between the senior commanders came close to open hostility at times. This distracted Eisenhower and led to a compromise that was to see the Allies defeated for the only time in the European campaign.

The Airborne divisions meanwhile focussed on the 10,000 replacements they were going to have to train, and a major re-organisation. Activated on 2 August the First Allied Airborne Army was to be the biggest ever formed, combining American, British and Polish assets, and commanded by Lieutenant General Lewis Brereton with British General 'Boy' Browning as deputy.

Brereton, who had planned the proposed parachute assaults during WWI, was an Air Force officer and staunch advocate of the effectiveness of air power. This apparently excellent qualification masked a lack of understanding of what happened once air power had delivered the soldiers to the battlefield. His deputy was an extremely able Guards officer who had been responsible for the formation and training of British glider and parachute forces. Not immune to idiosyncrasies he had also designed his own rather unique uniform. (Browning's other contribution to Airborne uniform, however, was the red beret. It has subsequently been adopted by airborne forces the world over, not least amongst them the US Airborne who wear it with pride to this day.)

Ridgway meanwhile had been promoted to command the US XVIII Airborne Corps, his deputy, Gavin, assuming command of the 82nd on 28 August. As part of the Change of Command ceremonies that month, Generals Eisenhower, Ridgway, Brereton and Gavin reviewed the 82nd. During that review Ike made the comment about 'owing you (the 82nd) a lot' and never a more prophetic word was spoken.

The components of the new force were:

- US XVIII Airborne Corps: US 17th, 82nd, and 101st Airborne Divisions
- I British Airborne Corps: 1st and 6th British Airborne Divisions, 1st Polish Independent Parachute Brigade, 52nd (Lowland) Division (Airportable)
- USAAF IX Troop Carrier Command
- Nos 38 and 46 Groups, RAF

Eisenhower eventually decided to give priority to Montgomery's 21st Army Group as it thrust through Belgium towards Holland, securing the Channel ports and overrunning V-2 sites that were dropping the world's first operational ballistic missiles on London. This priority was, however, to be temporary, for once the great port of Antwerp was in Allied hands, it would switch to Bradley's 12th Army Group for a direct attack across the Rhine.

Slightly to the surprise of all, Montgomery moved fast. Brussels was liberated on 3 September and the city of Antwerp, but not its vital sea approaches, the following day. By the 12th Monty's men were in Holland. During August and early September no less than 18 plans to speed the advance even more had been formulated, many involving the Airborne, only for these to be dropped, overtaken by the unexpectedly rapid advances on the ground. At this point, as British Lieutenant General Sir Brian Horrocks later commented 'We made the mistake of underestimating our enemy—a very dangerous thing to do when fighting the Germans.'

On 5 September Monty was offered the First Allied Airborne Army to speed his advance. His response was an uncharacteristically daring plan. An 'airborne carpet' was to be laid from Eindhoven to Arnhem with the objective of capturing vital bridges and securing a route for the British XXX Corps which would drive rapidly to cross the Rhine at the last one, Arnhem. Speed was of the essence, which made the plan risky. During the planning Browning is reputed to have made the famous comment about the attempt on Arnhem possibly being 'a bridge too far'.

The airborne part of the operation was to be Operation Market, whilst the ground assault became Operation Garden. It was set to begin on 17 September,

leaving little time for fine detail in the planning or the collection of up-to-date intelligence regarding German dispositions (and what intelligence there was, it transpired, was woefully inaccurate). Worse, there was insufficient co-ordination at the highest levels.

Briefly the plan was for the 101st Airborne to secure the first part of the corridor around Eindhoven. The 82nd was to seize the bridge across the Maas at Grave, a number of canal crossings, and the vital Nijmegen bridges across the Waal. One road and one rail, both were substantial enough to take armour and the only crossings for some 20 miles. High ground around Groesbeek was also to be occupied to block any German advance out of the Reichswald Forest. Finally the British were to jump on the last bridge in the chain, Arnhem. Theirs of course was the farthest point from relief.

The whole plan rested on the speed with which the armoured thrust on the ground could link up with the airborne troops and force the corridor. Once launched the plan would be obvious to the enemy and any delay would increase the risk to those holding the farthest parts of the 75 mile 'carpet'. The payoff, however, was a flanking of the Siegfried Line that would place the Allies close to Germany's industrial heartland of the Ruhr. Market-Garden had the potential to shorten the war.

Because there simply were not enough transports to lift this huge force in one go, the drops were to be incremental over three days. The good news, however, was that because the Allies enjoyed near total air superiority the assault would go in during daylight hours. This it was hoped (and subsequently proved) would reduce the scattering so prevalent in night drops. Lessons learnt in Normandy were also taken on board. Paratroopers were not going to be shot up before they hit the ground this time, they were going to jump with loaded weapons so they could come down blazing. The artillery was going to make its first parachute insertion, too, the 376th PFA jumping alongside Gavin's men.

As D-Day neared preparations went into overdrive. Every artillery and flak emplacement along the route was bombed and strafed from high, medium and low levels. B-17s, B-26s, American P-47 Thunderbolts and British Typhoons all added their firepower. Such was the Allied control of the skies that the Luftwaffe had no real counter and the Germans discerned no plan amongst all the other bombing.

As 1,545 transports and 478 gliders began loading with troops and materiel on the morning of the 17th there were the usual nerves for the newly trained and the studied nonchalance of their battle-hardened comrades. Much gallows humour centred on the 504th who were to jump on Grave. Some officers tried to fend it off by talking about 'Gravey' but to little avail amongst the unit wits (actually it is pronounced to rhyme with 'starve')

At 11.09hrs the take-offs began and the vast aerial armada headed in two streams towards Holland. First on the ground were the pathfinders who landed at 12.47hrs. Less than 15 minutes later Gavin, first out as ever, led the 505th down onto DZ 'N' just south of Groesbeek. Jumping with the infantry was the 376th PFA whose men had their ten 75mm pack howitzers assembled within minutes of landing. Moving 1,000 yards to the first gun line, the 376th was able to provide fire support to the 508th by 18.00hrs and was soon supported by the 456th who arrived by glider with jeeps and more artillery the next day.

Also arriving by glider in the 505th's area was General Browning and his HQ. Slightly to the north and east of Groesbeek Colonel Roy Lindquist's 508th jumped on DZ 'T', whilst on the left flank Rueben Tucker's 504th jumped on both sides of the bridge over the Maas River at Grave. This proved the most successful drop of the day as Tuckers' men quickly overran both ends of the bridge. The 52nd Troop

Above right: The journey—this map shows the track and waypoints on the northern and southern routes to Holland. (Based on drawings in the USAAF's Secret report on Operation Market Garden)

Below right: The landings—this map shows the drop zones used on 17 September. 505th PIR dropped on DZ 'O' near Grave. Grave bridge over the Maas was taken swiftly. 505th and 508th PIRs were dropped or landed at LZ 'N' and 'T' respectively, 456th Parachute FA Battalion landing on LZ 'N'. The artillery—75mm pack howitzers—was decisive in the early part of the battle, the only support for the infantry until Allied armour closed on the 19th. (Based on drawings in the USAAF's Secret report on Operation Market Garden)

NIJMEGEN
Map 4
Routes to Nijmegen

The Wash

BARKSTON
HEATH

SALTBY
COTTESMORE
FOLKINGHAM

SPANHOE

March
52˚ 33' 40" N – 00˚ 04' 10" E
Code "M"

Antigua
52˚ 08' 20" N
01˚ 36' 15" E
Code "A"

Tampa
51˚ 55' 55" N
02˚ 40' 00" E
Code "K"

Altu
51˚ 44' 00" N
00˚ 54' 25" E
Code "S"

Borneo
51˚ 22' 25" N
01˚ 25' 55" E
Code "B"

Miami
51˚ 19' 25" N
02˚ 13' 30" E
Code "M"

Catalina
51˚ 16' 20" N
05˚ 00' 20" E

Bermuda
50˚ 45' 15" N
03˚ 41' 30" E

Ellis IP
51˚ 38' 15" N
05˚ 18' 15" E

DZ "Y"   DZ "X"
ARNHEM
DZ "K" LG "G"
DZ "O"
DZ & LZ "T"
DZ & LZ "N"

Route No 1 Northern

Columbia
51˚ 38' 50" N
04˚ 05' 52" E

EINDHOVEN

Heghtel

ANTWERP

Route No 2 Southern

Duff
51˚ 01' 35" N
03˚ 41' 25" E

Delos
51˚ 06' 50" N
04˚ 53' 37" E

English Channel

Map 5
The Nijmegen drops

Waal

NIJMEGEN

Niel

B 10

Wijchen

B 9

Canal

B 8

Wyler

DZ & LZ "T"
508 PIR

Kranenburg

Donsbrugge

Groesbeek

DZ "O"
504 PIR

DZ & LZ "N"
505 PIR

504
PIR   Grave

Overasselt

Maas (Meuse)

Mook

456 PFA Bn

Gennep

Kessel

Left: C-47 full of paratroopers awaiting take-off, 17 September 1944. (via Real War Photos)

Right: The Nijmegen drop. This C-47, serial 2100833, is from the 439th Troop Carrier Group (squadron code L4). 'Chalk 3' was a stick of 14 men from Charlie Company, 307th Engineer Battalion, who took part in the Waal crossing. The aircraft also dropped para packs containing mine detectors, radios, BARs, tools, mines and explosives. Taken by the CO of the 439th (the wing of whose C-47 can be seen) the picture is made more interesting as everyone on the aircraft is known. 1-Lt Melvin Ullrick led the stick which consisted of S/Sgt Noel E. Morrison, Sgt William Kero, T/5 Russel S. Anderson, Pfcs Garo Kirkorian, Raymond H. Slocum, Carmen J. Western and Pvts Alexander S. Nemeth, Robert R. Freel, Joseph E. Jobora, Hutchel B. Stansbury, Raymond H. Geroux, James W. Pembleton and Howard Miller. The aircraft was piloted by 1-Lt Henry L. Harris with co-pilot 2-Lt Stephen V. Sajawies. Crew chief was S/Sgt Howard E. Gerard and Radio Operator T/Sgt Howard T. Love. (Col Charles Young).

Below left: DZ 'T' Groesbeek. A poor quality but historically interesting picture taken by one of two American war reporters who jumped with the troops that day. Col Roy Lindquist's 508th PIR are seen landing here. There are well over 100 parachutes visible in this shot indicating how tightly the formations of Dakotas flew. Comparison of this shot with one taken nearly 50 years later (inset) shows that certain things don't change. (US Army/inset Mike Verier)

Below right: Another view of the landings. (US Army)

Above: The drop was one of the biggest of WWII and extremely accurate—but not as accurate as this spring 1945 practice drop. (via Real War Photos)

Carrier Wing's after action report has a map showing where the actual drops were made in relation to the planned DZs. It shows all the drops were extremely accurate and, where the dots for the 504th do not match the DZ, there is a slightly sniffy note pointing out that this was at the unit commander's insistence!

This drop was at the time the biggest ever attempted, and it was not without its problems, the hung loads (including one or two paratroopers caught in the static lines), engine failures and flak damage were almost expected, but there were human costs, too. Serial A-9 of the 316th Troop Carrier Group (42 C-47s, 3 C-53s) dropped 677 men of the 504th and 270 parapacks on DZ 'O'. One aircraft had to land at Feltwell to discharge a paratrooper who had 'gone out of his mind'. Having done so it immediately re-joined the formation and completed the drop. On the return journey the same aircraft ditched in the Channel, all the crew being picked up by the air-sea rescue organisation.

Rather bizarrely, above this armada was a B-17 full of war correspondents and photographers calmly observing the operation for posterity, but not all were content with such a detached view, Serial A-7's manifest included the famous CBS commentator Ed Murrow, and his technician Mr Maselle who had insisted on being in a C-47 with the troops.

Once on the ground, Gavin quickly set about establishing the enemy's dispositions, with his Dutch liaison officer Captain Arie Bestebreurtje, soon in telephone contact with the Dutch resistance from a local house. The British paratroops were to regret their lack of Dutch liaison in the days that followed.

Groesbeek was also a railway junction, and during the night one train passed through the area unchallenged, a fact that apparently did not please Gavin (his testiness more than somewhat due to a painful back injury suffered during the jump). Ever willing to please their commander the troopers set about the next two with bazookas. One was carrying fuel for V-2s, the resultant spectacular explosion nearly taking the troopers with it.

By the end of D-Day, whilst all the landings had been successful, none of the main objectives of Market had been taken, and the armoured thrust had not even begun. The Allies, however, were committed and as D+1 dawned efforts were re-doubled. Three times that day Gavin's soldiers reported the bridge in their hands, but the German defences held and each time the Americans were forced to withdraw.

In the 82nd's sector the defensive perimeter was pretty thin and Gavin was finally forced to withdraw the 3rd/508th from attacking Nijmegen to prevent German counter-attacks from overrunning the glider LZs. With some difficulty they were cleared just in time for the gliders that arrived overhead around 14.00hrs.

Once again most of the gliders made an accurate landing despite heavy flak. This time the lift brought in the 319th and 320th GFA, and the 456th PFA plus the balance of the 307th Airborne Engineers, the 80th Airborne Anti-Aircraft Artillery and some medics. Materiel delivered included 30 howitzers, eight 57mm anti-tank guns and over 90 jeeps. Twenty minutes later a supply drop by 135 B-24 Liberators was also successfully made. Some 25 gliders overshot, some landing up to five miles inside Germany, but remarkably more than half the personnel involved eventually fought or infiltrated their way back to Allied lines.

By the end of the second day Major General Taylor's 101st Airborne and the British XXX Corps commanded by Horrocks had at last broken out from Eindhoven and were on their way to link up with the increasingly hard pressed 82nd. The bridges at Nijmegen were still in German hands, although engineers had managed to disable the demolition charges during the night so that at least they remained intact.

On the 19th (D+2) the Guards Armoured Division, spearheading XXX Corps, finally linked up with Gavin's men at Grave bridge, the leading elements making contact with the 504th at 08.20hrs. With no time lost, the 2nd/505th was placed under the command of the Guards and the tanks and infantry moved towards Nijmegen. Initially they met only light resistance and moved into the town, taking the post office, which was rumoured to contain demolition apparatus for the bridges. Short of their objectives, however, both columns were stopped by heavy enemy fire which knocked out the lead tanks. Flanking attacks by Grenadier Guards on the road bridge, and a combined force of grenadiers and paratroops on the rail bridge failed to make headway and by nightfall a stalemate had been reached. Elsewhere the 508th was still fending off probing attacks by the Germans on its thinly stretched defensive lines.

Gavin and Browning had become increasingly anxious for the British paras at Arnhem, who would not be relieved unless the bridges were carried. Gavin concluded that the only way to break the stalemate was to get troops across the river and flank the defenders. To this end he requested that Horrocks' engineers bring up their boats from the rear, planning that the 504th would cross at 08.00hrs the next morning, under cover of an artillery barrage.

In the event the boats were late, the vehicles making very slow progress on the one congested road open to them. For the moment, however, Gavin's immediate attention was on Mook and Beek, heavily under attack by the 6th *Fallschirmjäger* Division—no second rate formation. Leaving to take personal charge of the situation Gavin supervised the counter-attacks. In Mook the 505th re-took the town street by street, whilst at Beek the 508th, who had been asked to hold the

Netherlands Orange Lanyard

HQ and HQ Company, 82d Airborne Division
Cited in Department of Army General Orders 43 of 19 December 1950:

Considering that the outstanding performance of duty of the 82d Airborne Division, United States Army, during the airborne operations and the ensuing fighting actions in the central part of the Netherlands in the period from 17 September to 4 October has induced HER MAJESTY, THE QUEEN, to decorate its divisional color with the Military Order of William, degree of the knight of the fourth class, considering also, that is desirable for each member of the personnel of the 82nd Airborne Division, United States Army, who took part in the aforesaid operations, to possess a lasting memento of this glorious struggle; decrees: that each member of the personnel of the 82d Airborne Division, United States Army, who took part in the operations in the area of Nijmegen in the period from 17 September to 4 October 1944 is allowed to wear the Orange Lanyard of the Royal Netherlands Army.

Above: The ubiquitous 'Jeep' (a contraction of 'GP' as in 'General Purpose') provided most of the Airborne's mobility. This one is the Divisional G-1 jeep (note the star plate over the 82A/B stencil on the bumper) awaiting its passenger at the 508th's Harness CP. (US Army)

position if possible, went on the attack and that night re-took the town, pursuing the Germans all the way back to the Rhine.

The Waal crossings

When the British canvas boats finally arrived, the troopers set to preparing them. There were 26 assault boats, holding ten men each. It was nearly 15.00hrs before this small force pushed out into the fast current of the Waal led by Captains Thomas M. Burris and Carl W. Koppel.

Preceded by rocket-firing Typhoons, a ferocious artillery barrage had been laid down ahead of the assault, along with smoke to try and give some cover. When reports reached German commanders they initially dismissed the idea of an assault across the river—they simply did not think it could be done. The German troops on the spot, however, some 400–600 soldiers, lost no time in opening up on the boats as the smoke screen was blown away, leaving the frantically paddling Americans exposed in mid-river.

Terrible carnage was wrought as the troopers struggled against the current, so much so that only 13 of the boats returned. Those that did get ashore, however, sought vengeance. The ferocity of their attack quite overwhelmed the Germans, who faltered in the face of screaming troopers coming at them with bayonets and grenades. Seeing the destruction of the boats some troopers on the far shore simply took bandoliers of ammunition and their rifles and swam across (which says much for the physical condition of paratroopers). Tanks acting as artillery pounded the Germans from across the river in an attempt to support the troopers on the far side.

Gradually (some six return trips were necessary) the 1st and 3rd/504th got their men across and drove the Germans eastwards. First the railway and then the road bridge was cleared. The 504th suffered over 100 casualties during this action, but the Germans lost four times as many men.

Whilst the hand to hand fighting for the northern shore was going on the Grenadiers and the 505th hit the southern end of the bridge. By 17.00hrs the Germans were routed and the 82nd had control of the north end of the bridges. The

Right: Men of the 50th Anti-Tank Battalion pause at a roadside shrine in Belgium during December 1944. Left to right: Pvt Chas A. Badeaux, T/5 Theodore B. Sohoski and Pvt John H. Bogdan. (T/5 Emil Edgren, US Army)

first tanks of the Grenadiers, supported by the 2nd/505th were across by 19.00hrs. It took some time to secure the vast road bridge fully, several Germans being winkled out from hiding places under its structure as late as the following morning.

As British and American troops began to stream across the bridge and dig in, the Germans were re-grouping. The counter-attack came the next day (21st) at noon. Supported by tanks it nearly succeeded in dislodging the Allies. During this action Private John Towle used his bazooka to drive off two tanks and destroy a house being used as a strong point before succumbing to enemy fire. His heroic action earned a second Medal of Honor for the division.

Bad weather had meanwhile delayed the arrival of the 325th Glider Infantry and Gavin was reduced to forming an ad hoc battalion from 450 glider pilots who released some paratroopers for action by guarding the divisions' growing number of German prisoners. Fortunately Gavin's foresight in making sure that there was artillery with the first lift meant that the thinly spread paratroopers at least had some support.

Support was sadly lacking in other areas. A terrible lack of co-ordination at the highest levels meant that the Luftwaffe was able to get in amongst the transports and attack both ground and air targets. The Allies, having started from a position of air superiority, failed to maintain it. The consequences of this for the encircled British paras were all too obvious.

Despite the best efforts of the Airborne soldiers it did not prove possible to relieve the British paratroops at Arnhem. The Poles, delayed by weather, were finally committed but the first wave of gliders arrived unescorted and was cut to pieces on the LZ. The full story is beyond the scope of this narrative but of the 10,300 men who jumped on Arnhem only 2,587 made it back to Allied lines. Montgomery's plan had indeed proved too ambitious.

Market-Garden as planned was abandoned by Eisenhower on the 22nd (D+5) but the fighting went on unabated and the men of the 82nd found themselves serving as 'legs' under General Horrocks (who they regarded as a good commander). The battle for Nijmegen was not over as far as the Germans were concerned and they continued to attack the bridges with their newly acquired jets, the Me 262 and Ar 234, as well as swimmers with mines.

The 325th finally arrived on D+6, 3,385 troops being delivered into the 82nd's area, and an airhead was established at an abandoned Luftwaffe field near Grave where supplies could be flown in. This also permitted the repatriation of the badly needed glider pilots. Gavin, meanwhile, finally got his second star and promotion to major general.

The 82nd was to be given no rest for, despite protests from Brereton, Montgomery had persuaded Eisenhower to keep it in the line along with the 101st. The 82nd remained in combat until November suffering more casualties than during Market-Garden itself. Finally it was relieved and sent to the rear for some much-needed rest.

Based near Reims the 'resting' paratroopers kept in fighting trim by scrapping with the 101st at any opportunity and vying for the favours of local girls. Conscious of the possibility of their being summoned for fire-brigade duties, Gavin made sure that full stocks of ammunition and supplies were to hand even though the division was supposed to be in reserve. His prudence was justified.

Above: Pfc Richard Stafford of the light machine gun platoon, HQ Company 1st Battalion 508th PIR at Nijmegen. Picture was taken on the Dammen van Poldesveldtweg. Stafford was the first trooper to walk down the street. The weapon is a water-cooled .30 cal. Browning, the M1917A1. (via 82nd AB Division Museum)

THE BATTLE OF THE BULGE

Whilst the 82nd was re-fitting the Allies pushed on. On 8 November the US Third Army began its drive to breach the German West Wall defensive line, whilst on the 16th the First Army began the Hürtgen Forest campaign. The results of this latter were to become all too apparent to the 82nd in the spring. In the meantime the Germans were already planning a massive counter-offensive in the west. By the time the US First Army began attacking the River Roer Dams on 13 December the Germans were already massing in their forward assembly areas.

Much of the Allied campaign in Europe was characterised by poor intelligence (or, more accurately, a failure to recognise information for what it was). Such was the case with the German assault in the Ardennes in late 1944. Despite considerable reconnaissance information clearly showing troop movements and supply build-ups that presaged an armoured assault, the Allies were caught completely flat-footed in the Ardennes. Quite apart from intelligence failings the Allies were seriously over-stretched. They had failed to predict the heavy losses of the autumn and were short of both men and equipment; worse they felt that the Germans were already beaten and had allowed a certain degree of complacency to set in.

The Germans on the other hand were not about to admit defeat, Hitler's ambitious plan called for an armoured drive that would reach Antwerp, splitting the allied armies in two. The Germans were, moreover, used to the terrain—after all they had used this route of attack in 1870, 1914 and 1940. Combined with parachute assault in the rear, and the confusion that the 'Greif' commandos (using captured equipment and wearing American uniforms) would cause, the offensive had a real chance of success against the small number of 'green' troops holding the more than 80-mile line that would be attacked.

There were many flaws in the plan, which was clearly too ambitious for the resources available. Many of Hitler's senior commanders argued against it in fact, but to no avail. They had also not reckoned with the resilience of the ordinary American soldiers. They may have been green, in under-strength units and ill-prepared, but they held out long enough for the Airborne divisions (the only reserve SHAEF had) to arrive and plug the gaps. The Airborne in its turn stopped the German advance, refusing to surrender in the face of overwhelming odds, until Patton's Third Army and Hodges' First Army finally arrived.

The operation known to the Germans as *Wacht am Rhein* and to history as the Battle of the Bulge was to prove the US Army's biggest battle of WWII, and cost it 80,987 men killed, wounded or missing.

The assault begins

At 05.30hrs on 16 December the German attack fell without warning on the American front. Artillery and mortar barrages preceded infantry assaults backed by armour. To their credit the front line troops, overrun in some places, turned and fought, slowing the Germans who had reckoned on punching through and driving relentlessly west. The defences in the Losheim Gap began to give, but elsewhere the Sixth Panzer Army made little progress against the US 2nd and 99th Divisions. Fifth Panzer Army was also making less headway than planned against the 28th Division.

The situation was extremely tenuous, however, and the American command quickly realised that the thin line of troops in place could not hold for long. That night the Losheim Gap was breached, leaving the 106th Division almost surrounded. The following morning Obersturmbannführer Joachim Peiper's 1st SS

Above: 'Somewhere in Belgium' (it was actually taken around Christmas day, between Bra and Frature). This photo of an 82nd soldier running to a new scouting position, Thompson in hand, was a source of inspiration for General Gavin who kept it in his office. When, in 1958, the soldier was eventually identified as Earl E. Potter, Gavin wrote that it 'epitomised something fundamental; the spirit the individual has that motivates him in the middle of danger to take every risk and do the right thing is far more important to us than all the equipment that we can buy.' (82nd Airborne Museum)

Panzer Division captured Bullingen, and the 18th Volksgrenadier Division captured the Schönberg Bridge completing the encirclement. Later that afternoon Peiper's SS troops massacred 85 unarmed American prisoners in a field near Malmédy.

Still thinking that the German attack was little more than a spoiling operation designed to divert troops from the Roer dams, the Allied High Command, having released the 7th and 10th Armored Divisions from reserve, relaxed. Bradley and Eisenhower spent the evening playing bridge. Finally, late that evening, it sank in that a major incursion was underway and that help was needed fast—at last the alarm bells were ringing. The only reserves available were the re-fitting Airborne divisions, the 82nd and the 101st. Eisenhower released them immediately.

Having received the alert at around midnight, Gavin's foresight in having ammunition and supplies ready was quickly repaid. The 82nd was moving towards the front by 07.00hrs. This was partly achieved by side-stepping the Army's ponderous bureaucracy—the trucks needed were in SHAEF's huge motor pool and the written orders needed for their release were certainly not available in the middle of the night. Undaunted, the paratroopers' senior NCOs simply 'arrested' any rear echelon type who dared to challenge them, taking some 500 trucks and virtually kidnapping 300 drivers. By the time the 101st arrived on a similar mission there were only cattle trucks left.

This somewhat unconventional approach had two consequences, the 82nd arrived at the front line in time to block the Germans—24 hours later and the battle would have been very different in outcome. Secondly their original orders were for Bastogne, but because the division was already on the move they were changed for Werbomont (further north) and the following 101st directed to Bastogne instead. (Gavin had overall command of XVIII Airborne Corps briefly as Ridgway was in England and the 101st CO, Taylor, was in America.)

By the 19th the Germans were pressing on the whole front. The vital crossroads at Bastogne and St Vith were holding but only just, both being all but surrounded. Meanwhile the 82nd fanned out from Werbomont to take up a defensive line along the Salm River, finding itself in a similar position to that they had held in Holland—German forces to their north, south and east. Such was the Airborne spirit, however, that the 82nd generally held German forces in its area as being in far greater trouble than it was. The optimism was not shared by all, for that afternoon some 7–8,000 American troops surrendered on the Schnee Eifel.

Cited in the Order of the Day of the Belgian Army for actions in Belgium and Germany
HQ and HQ Company, 82nd Airborne Division
Cited in Department of the Army General Orders 43 of19 December 1950:

After having excelled in defensive warfare at the banks of the Salm and the Ambleve, and having repelled successfully the repeated attacks of the best German shock troops, the 82nd Airborne Division with the 508th Parachute Infantry Regiment attached, in spite of the extreme cold and excessively deep snow, went on the offensive themselves and advanced to the German border, capturing 2,500 German prisoners, including five battalion commanders. This fighting was extremely valorous as the organic composition of the division handicapped the unit considerably, not having at their disposal, as any other Infantry Division would have, heavy weapons to support their attack. During 23 days, under most painful and adverse conditions, the veterans of the 82nd Airborne Division did not cease to give a wonderful example of courage and heroism, exemplifying their fighting spirit by several remarkably brilliant actions. By its valor, the division wrote another page in heroic annals of Allied airborne troops and rendered an important service to Belgium and to the Allied cause by establishing the necessary basis for the new pursuit of the enemy toward the Rhine River.

Left: An interesting shot from December 1944 simply captioned 'two recon boys in the Bulge.' Their jeep has been turned into a scout car by the installation of improvised armour and a .50 cal machine gun (a formidable weapon, still in use today). The rear wheels have been fitted with snow chains and the vehicle appears to have been painted white in a concession to local operating conditions. Appropriate clothing, however, was by no means universal as can be seen from the crew. (US Army)

Above: An improvised defensive position in the Odrimont sector (Belgium) provides cover for S/Sgt Charles O. Marible (left) and Pfc Louis E. Jenkins of the 325th Glider Regiment. Aside from the .30 cal machine gun, note that rifle and grenades are also close to hand. (T/5 Norbuth, US Army)

Below: Men of the 508th PIR with their jeeps in the Ardennes—a picture that gives some inkling of the terrible conditions the soldiers had to cope with during the winter campaign. (US Army)

Gavin had been ordered by the now returned Ridgway to hold the widest possible area. Consequently the 325th was deployed to Barvaux in the west, and Grandmenil and Mouhan to the south. The 505th initially went to Habiemont, then on the following day further east to Basse-Bodeaux and Trois Ponts. The 504th also moved east over a couple of days, first to Rahier, then on to Cheneaux and Trois Ponts. Finally the 508th was sent to the heights of Their Dumont. As the divisional artillery arrived it was deployed to support the paras and glidermen.

Gavin was in no doubt that his troops would soon encounter German armour. This time, however, the 82nd was better prepared, for not only had the battle-hardened troopers evolved effective tactics for dealing with tanks, they also had some new tricks up their sleeves.

Throughout the war the Americans had suffered from poor anti-tank weapons, the 57mm gun and the infantry bazooka having little effect on newer German tanks, which also out-gunned the standard Allied tank, the Sherman. The wily paratroopers, however, had come across a considerable quantity of German Panzerfaust hand-held anti-tank rockets in Holland. Gavin himself was seriously impressed with this weapon and they were put to good use in the Ardennes. His gunners had also noted the British discarding sabot round for the 57mm (6-pounder) gun with its far greater penetrating power and traded whatever they could for some carefully hoarded rounds they were now to make good use of.

The 504th in fact quickly made use of its Panzerfausts. On the afternoon of the 20th it encountered a battalion of the 2nd SS Panzer Grenadiers and after fierce hand-to-hand combat captured over a dozen flakwagons and a battery of 105mm howitzers (prompting the unit wits to call themselves the '504th Parachute Armored Regiment'). It is perhaps fortunate for the 38 prisoners they took that afternoon that the paratroopers were not aware that they were from the battalion who had perpetrated the Malmédy massacre.

By now, however, St Vith and Bastogne were completely cut off and their survival depended on the 82nd preventing a German crossing of the Salm River. Around dawn on the 21st the 1st SS Panzer Division fell on the positions of Lt Colonel Ben Vandervoort's 2nd/505th. Calmly declining Gavin's offer of reinforcements, Vandervoort's men held off the best the Germans had.

The 82nd's front now extended some 25 miles, and the following morning the 325th on the right flank was assaulted by an armoured force and forced to withdraw some distance, although not before the 82nd's 75mm artillery had inflicted severe losses on the Germans. The German advance was halted by the engineers blowing a bridge, and the timely arrival of the 325th's reserve battalion.

Whilst this was going on General McAuliffe of the 101st was delivering his famous 'Nuts!' response to the German call for the surrender of Bastogne. St Vith on the other hand had to be abandoned. The 508th, which was holding the corridor through which its heroic defenders were retreating, found itself under attack by the 9th SS Panzer Division.

By the following day, with retreating troops passing through its positions, the regiment was under attack by three SS Divisions plus other German units. Despite the US 3rd Armored Division pulling out (which exposed their right flank) the paratroopers held out through the night of 23/24 December until tanks of the 9th Armored Division were finally assigned to give them some support.

The 82nd had bought the time that the besieged defenders of Bastogne needed. Re-supplied by air, the 101st fought off a massive attack on Christmas Day and held out until the 26th when Patton's 4th Armored Division finally broke through and lifted the siege.

Meanwhile, on Christmas Eve, now under command of Monty's 21st Army Group, the 82nd received orders much to its disgust to withdraw to more compact defensive lines, By Christmas Day it was in place. German probes of the new lines were not long coming and on the 27th a massive attack by the 9th SS Panzers was repulsed with some difficulty by the 504th and 508th. This attack, however, seemed to mark the end of serious German offensive action which simply ran out of steam. The initiative was about to pass to the Allies.

Above: An airborne bulldozer of the 307th Engineer Battalion pushes a German tank destroyer aside on a narrow forest road whilst troopers wait anxiously to get on. (US Army)

Counter-attack

On 3 January the Allies went on the attack. On the first day the 82nd, augmented by the 551st Parachute Battalion and the 517th Parachute Infantry Regiment, and supported by the 740th Tank Battalion, lost no time in assaulting the Germans. The 740th was much respected by the paras—unlike many armoured formations it shared the Airborne's aggressive spirit. Between them they overran the 62nd Volksgrenadier Division and the 9th SS Panzers, taking some 2,500 prisoners. To their incredulity they were then ordered to stop. Monty's other troops lacked the drive of these two élite units and had to catch up—there was much bitching in the ranks.

Unleashed again on the 8th the 82nd pushed on through Vielsalm, where divisional artillery caught and decimated a German column of 35 vehicles and 500 troops at a crossroads. Moving on to the Salm River it quickly re-took the territory relinquished a couple of weeks earlier. During this drive 1st Sergeant Leonard Funk of the 508th, in an action that would have been incredible if Hollywood had written it, deservedly won the division's final Medal of Honor of WWII. The 82nd finally received some hard-earned rest when the 75th Infantry Division relieved it on the 9th allowing the paras back some 20 miles to Chevron.

During this brief respite some troopers managed to wangle leave and get into the usual trouble (that side of military life remains little changed). Towards the end of the war a slightly more relaxed attitude allowed some troopers to furlough in more exotic places such as Nice on the French Mediterranean coast, although even in such idyllic surroundings high spirits led to the odd scrape. One group, who had 'borrowed' an MP jeep for a couple of days, was finally rounded up and triumphantly incarcerated by the aggrieved owners of the vehicle whilst higher authority was summoned. Locking paratroopers in a second floor room with open windows was not the smartest move, however. The miscreants were long gone by the time the officer arrived!

Below: Major General James Gavin directs troops in Belgium, 28 January 1945. (via 82nd Airborne Museum)

Above: Men of the HQ Company, 508th PIR take a break during the march to assembly areas, La Avenanters, Belgium, 6 January 1945. A variety of improvised winter dress employed by the troopers is evident. The trooper in the foreground appears to be wearing a British leather jerkin. (US Army)

Into the dragon's teeth

Early on the morning of 27 January the 82nd again began a move back into combat. Boarding trucks and heading east it was to spearhead the assault on the last great German defensive barrier, the Siegfried Line. This formidable defence stretched along the German border from the Waal to the Rhine, belts of bunkers, trenches, machine-gun nests, minefields and dragon's teeth were tiered to provide overlapping fire support and were over a mile in depth. Virtually impervious to artillery or aerial bombardment by the weapons of the day they presented a formidable obstacle.

At 04.00hrs on 2 February the All Americans led the assault on the West Wall destroying bunkers systematically as they went, often with the Germans' own weapon, the Panzerfaust. Once through they seized the German towns of Udenbreth and Neuhof, as well as the Hertserott Heights. To their disgust no real effort was made to exploit the breach they had made.

There followed a few days rest and re-fit before the troopers were back in combat, this time in the dreadful conditions of the Hürtgen Forest. As mentioned earlier the US forces had tried to take this ground the previous autumn in an operation that Gavin was to criticise heavily post-war. It had turned into a meat grinder. Seven divisions had lost 33,000 men to no avail.

What awaited the 82nd in the early thaw of 1945 was sickening even to hardened troopers. As the snow began to melt countless thousands of bodies from the winter debacle began to emerge. The 82nd found evidence of wounded soldiers simply abandoned and left to die at an aid station. To a unit that prided itself on caring for its wounded this was appalling, more so that such an act was perpetrated by their own side.

Between 8 and 17 February the 82nd pushed through Kommerscheidt and then into Schmidt before reaching the swollen Roer River (the Germans had succeeded in blowing the dam). Fortunately for the 82nd the proposed assault crossing was cancelled, the division having received orders to return to France, with its long winter war finally over.

ON TO BERLIN

The Ardennes battle had taken a terrible toll on the US forces, and very nearly split the Allied High Command (which of course had been Hitler's intention). It had however, cost the Germans more, 220,000 casualties, including the last really effective troops they possessed, and nearly 1,500 tanks and armoured vehicles that their increasingly pressed industries simply could not replace.

As the net closed round Germany from both the east and the west the 82nd was back at camps around Sissone-Suippes near Épernay in France. Gear and clothing badly needed replacement, and the troopers needed rest and good food. Otherwise the war ground relentlessly on. The 9th Armored Division had captured the bridge at Remagen intact and was across the Rhine on 7 March,

Meanwhile the usual potential uses for the Airborne were dreamed up by the generals and the rumour mill in equal measure. One old suggestion was less far-fetched than might be thought, for as far back as November 1944 Brereton had been asked to plan for a potential drop on Berlin. This was to be an operation that was to become an 82nd speciality post-war, the airfield take-down. Accordingly the paratroopers practised. Even on practice jumps some injuries were inevitable, but on one particular occasion, a Dakota that had just discharged its troopers suffered what appeared to be a propeller runaway and dived straight into the stick in front of it, taking five men to their death.

The Berlin jump was never to take place, since possibly for the first time in the war the 82nd was actually being held back to preserve its highly trained troops. The reasons, however, were entirely cynical. Unbeknown to Gavin the division was earmarked for the invasion of Japan, an assault which could well mean the sacrifice of the Airborne to achieve the aim.

Consequently it was the US 17th and the British 6th Airborne Divisions who made the last major drop of the war, Operation Varsity, on 24 March. Sent to to secure a bridgehead near Duisburg on the east bank of the Rhine the paras showed they had learned the lessons of Holland. In a little over two hours 1,696 aircraft and gliders landed 21,680 troopers. Losses were significant but the armour linked up the same day and the objective was secured.

Above: Colonel Charles Billingslea commanded the 325th Glider Regiment during the Battle of the Bulge. (82nd Airborne Museum)

The 82nd finally left the Sissone-Suippes area on 31 March, moving by road and rail to take up positions around the devastated German city of Cologne. There they found themselves guarding some 10,000 Russian slave labourers and PoWs abandoned by the retreating Germans, in addition to occupation duties. Whilst they were not supposed to be in 'combat' the troopers saw no reason for not conducting aggressive night patrols into German-held territory across the Rhine, or exchanging fire with the other side when possible. Off duty the men found it equally difficult to resist the charms of the local girls, despite this being technically 'fraternisation' which was forbidden.

Below: Men of the 508th PIR process German prisoners on 3 January 1945. (US Army)

The patrols across the Rhine became a major incursion on 6 April when a company of the 504th occupied the town of Hitdorf for nearly 24 hours. With the aid of reinforcement by another company they held off counter-attacks by 'seriously pissed'* German infantry and Tiger tanks. By the time the two companies withdrew the Germans had suffered some 200 casualties and drawn so many men from other positions that 13 miles away American forces broke through the resultant thinned lines—another good day for the Airborne.

By mid-April the Allied advance had slowed at the last major obstacle, the Elbe. Slated to cross this were the 82nd, along with 7th Armored and 8th Infantry, together with the British 6th Airborne. Accordingly the troopers once more boarded trucks for the front. During the journey they witnessed much of the devastation and destruction of the once great Reich.

On 23 April Soviet forces reached Berlin.

By the night of 28 April the 505th was at the banks of the Elbe and preparing for the crossing. Germans could be seen digging in on the other side but appeared somewhat half-hearted—few wanted to die for an already lost cause. The following night the collapsible boats were brought up and at 01.00hrs on the 29th the 505th surged across near the hamlet of Blekede, taking the Germans completely by surprise and encountering only sporadic resistance. The 504th followed and by noon the following day, despite a fierce artillery barrage, a pontoon had been

Above: Men of 504th PIR march through Cheneux, Belgium, 22 December 1944. (via Real War Photos)

constructed and the 82nd was across in force. That same day Hitler committed suicide in Berlin. 1 May found the troopers of the 82nd driving deeper into German territory with their preferred support, the 740th Tank Battalion.

Throughout the European fighting the paras had regarded tankers with some disdain, indeed they had suffered in the Ardennes when tanks 'cut and ran' instead of supporting them. Consequently when, on 29 December, Lt Colonel George K. Rubel had reported to the 505th that he was there to assist them he received a frankly hostile response. 'Tanks,' he was told, were 'more of a liability than an asset, they can't keep up with our troops.' Somewhat rankled by this, Rubel assured the paras that he would keep up if 'your guys get up off the ground and fight.' Within the hour infantry and tankers had surprised each other and hostility had changed to mutual respect. So it remained in May as the troopers of the 82nd pushed across Germany riding on the 740th's tanks.

Even so they never ceased to amaze the uninitiated. One newly arrived tank commander radioed his CO that he could not see the infantry following him—he was advised to look to the front for the 82nd. A little later on he again radioed that troopers were now passing him on bicycles. Shortly after that a horse and buggy with seven or eight troopers passed him. Later still, to his utter incredulity, he reported some 20 troopers on horseback rounding up Germans. Briefly formed that day the '505th Parachute Cavalry Regiment' continued to spearhead for the tanks.

Reaching Ludwigslust that night, the paras began to encounter increasing numbers of Germans fleeing westwards to avoid capture by the Russians. The culmination of this was a unique event in American military history, the surrender of an entire army to the 82nd. On 3 May Lieutenant General von Tippelskirch surrendered his Twenty-first Army of some 150,000 men, 2,000 vehicles and all their equipment to the paras. For them at least the war was over. On the same day patrols from the 82nd met Russians from VIII Mechanised Corps at Grabow.

Meanwhile other patrols had made a grim discovery just outside the town, the concentration camp at Wobelein. That night the mayor of Ludwigslust, who had been diverting rations intended for the prisoners to his own people, shot his wife and daughter before committing suicide. Although it was a small camp by German standards, the men of the 82nd were deeply shocked by the inhumanity and deprivation they found. Despite their best efforts many of the inmates were too weak to be saved. Shock was soon replaced by anger with the local townspeople and surviving German officers were made to dig graves.

That the German people might confront their complicity in such atrocity 200 bodies were laid out by these graves, dug in the town square, and the entire population forced to view them and pay some respect to those so grievously treated so close to their comfortable homes. Three chaplains from different denominations then held a memorial service at which the locals were left in no doubt of their responsibilities.

Many of the townspeople had simply refused to acknowledge what the Nazis were doing on their very doorstep, worse, many of the prisoners at Wobelein were 'political', including people from most of the occupied countries of Europe who had in some way offended the regime. For some the shame was too much to bear, and there was a rash of suicides following the memorial service.

The Russians
On the 5th contact was made with the main Russian formations. At first there was much back slapping and hand-shaking, a good deal of it for the benefit of those we would now call 'the media'. The 82nd attempted to socialise but quickly found that the Russian capacity for drink was almost limitless. Worse, the Russians were an undisciplined bunch concerned only with rape and pillage of the local population. Within days fraternisation was forbidden and all the appalled troopers could do was try to come between the locals and marauding bands of Russian soldiery whenever they could.

At midnight on 7 May Germany surrendered, and the 8th, VE Day, was celebrated throughout Europe with great euphoria. The men of the 82nd, many of whom were already on leave, began to think of home.

On 1 June the division returned to France where the troops began to wonder about Japan. Any campaign against the fanatical Japanese promised to be long and bloody in the extreme. Reports from Okinawa of heavy fighting and high casualties did nothing to calm their (entirely justified) fears that sooner or later they would once again find themselves at the sharp end. But then on 6 August a lone B-29, the *Enola Gay*, released a single weapon at 31,600 feet over a city called Hiroshima. In a blinding flash 52 seconds later world history changed forever.

OCCUPATION

The men of the 82nd were not to go home just yet. In August and September they were moved to be part of the occupation force in Berlin. Like many élite units their elan meant that they could bull as well as they could fight. During the spectacular VJ Day parade at Templehof Airport a special guard was laid on for General Patton. The proud troopers with their white cravats and spit-shined boots so impressed him that he commented, 'In all my years in the Army, and of all the honor guards I've seen, the 82nd Berlin Honor guard is the best', thus bestowing on the All Americans another sobriquet, 'America's Guard of Honor'.

Berlin was not all parades. There were jumps on the airport, as much for the benefit of the Russians as for continued training, and police duties in the shattered city. Once again the troopers found themselves trying to control the worst excesses of the Russians, who had taken to systematic looting. In particular they were boarding refugee trains at the last station before the American sector and robbing

Above: Company B, 325th Glider Regiment, in Belgium, 28 January 1945. The white snow clothing is a mixture of snow suits and white capes and hoods. (via Real War Photos)

Below: Rotating back to rest areas after a spell in the front line, 22 December 1944. (via Real War Photos)

Above: Crews check out an M24 Chaffee, 19 January 1945. Chafees were introduced into the ETO in December 1944 and was well liked by its crews. Thinly armoured, they were used well into the 1950s nearly 4,500 being produced up to June 1945. Light reconnaissance vehicles were used by 82nd Airborne postwar, the M551 Sheridan—the only airdroppable tank—seeing service until the late 1990s, including the Gulf War. (via Real War Photos)

the occupants of anything of value. Even gold teeth were ripped out and anyone protesting was beaten or killed, with no exception made for age or infirmity either.

The trains would arrive in the American sector with several dead and many injured. This daily occurrence greatly angered the troopers who were powerless to intervene. Eventually their anger reached General Gavin who went personally to witness the situation. Having passed through a particularly harrowing train load of injured and dead refugees his party came upon the perpetrators roughing up an old lady. As the Russians ran off laughing Gavin had to be restrained from shooting them himself.

Orders were thereafter changed. American guards were authorised to challenge and arrest anyone caught in such acts. Should they refuse to submit a warning shot was to be fired. If they still did not stop the guards were authorised to shoot them. Shortly after that three Russians made the mistake of thinking they could outrun an 82nd marksman. It was not long before the attacks ceased.

For the majority of the 82nd the closing months of 1945 were to see them gradually shipped home (the US Army operated a points system, those with the longest service—and therefore the most points—went first). By Christmas most of the division was back in the States.

TRIPLE NICKLE—THE 555TH

There is an often-overlooked part of the 82nd Airborne's history during the 1940s that nevertheless shaped the development of the US Army as it is today.

During WWII US forces were segregated. Through ignorance and prejudice America's black people were only allowed to serve in separate formations, often in second line roles. Even so, where they were allowed to show their mettle, black soldiers fought with bravery and skill every bit the match of their white contemporaries.

Encouraged by President Roosevelt, the McCoy Commission (named after the Secretary for War John T. McCoy) recommended in December 1943 that a test platoon of black paratroopers be formed, and this was activated on the 30th of that month as the *555th Parachute Test Platoon. (The * prefix was used by the Army to designate what was then known as a 'colored' unit.) Inevitably, the men of the 555th called themselves the 'Triple Nickles', with 'Nickles' deliberately misspelt, a unit tradition.

It was not made easy for them—just to get in the platoon the soldiers had to be better than the best. Senior NCOs had to sacrifice their stripes if they wanted in Training was conducted at Fort Benning, Georgia, a location where prejudice was endemic and overt. Despite all the obstacles placed in their way 17 of the 20 men gained their wings. It is worth noting that in percentage terms that is a much higher success rate than is ever achieved today.

From the beginning the Nickles carried themselves with great dignity; they knew that they were pioneers, there to prove that it both could and should be done and they were not going to buckle in the face of any provocation. From this cadre grew first a company and then a battalion. In July 1944 the unit moved from Fort Benning to Camp Mackall, North Carolina. On 25 November the unit was re-organised and re-designated as the *555th Parachute Infantry Battalion. The soldiers continued to train hard, anxious to get to Europe and avenge the German insult to athlete Jesse Owen at the 1936 Olympics. This was not to be, however. Despite being combat ready, and despite the massive losses suffered by the Airborne in Normandy, Holland and the Ardennes, the nearest they got to combat was helping to pack parachutes for the Normandy invasion.

When at last secret orders were received in March 1945 sending the Triple Nickles to Camp Pendleton in Oregon it was assumed they were headed for Japan, training in demolitions and EOD (Explosive and Ordnance Disposal) giving some credence to the rumour factory. The mission was to be called Operation Firefly.

Attached to the 9th Service Command, the paratroopers soon found that they had been 'volunteered' as smoke jumpers to augment the few crazy guys who jumped into trees for the US Forestry Service. The reason for this, and the EOD training, was one of the most bizarre attacks of any war, Japanese balloon bombs.

Lacking the ability to attack the US in any substantive way the Japanese came up with a number of bizarre schemes including a submarine aircraft carrier (intended to attack the Panama Canal). The concept of the balloon bombs was simple, hang incendiaries from balloons which would reach high enough altitudes for the prevailing winds to carry them across America. A simple

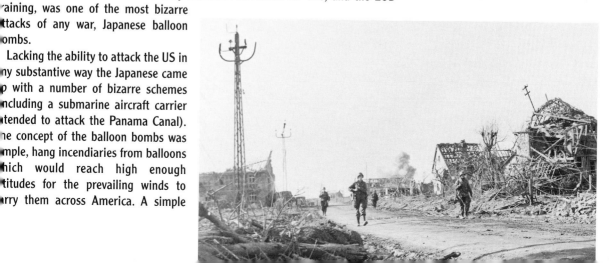

Right: Immaculately turned out and with bayonets fixed, the 82nd parades through Berlin at a victory ceremony. (82nd Airborne Museum)

clockwork release would then drop the weapons which would then start forest or crop fires. Great precision was not necessary—America is a big target—and bombs were scattered from Canada to Mexico, one falling as far away as Boise, Idaho.

The majority of the bombs, however, came down in the north-western forests, On 6 May 1945 a lady called Elsie Mitchell was on a fishing trip with five kids in Oregon, and they became the first victims of the bombs when a device they had found exploded.

This incident, and others where bits of balloon and equipment with Japanese writing on were found, prompted the Forestry Service to ask for help from the Army. Great secrecy was maintained at the time for fear of both the panic that might ensue amongst a population not used to being attacked, and backlash attacks on the Japanese-American population. Not mentioned was the far greater fear that these weapons could be used to dispense chemical or biological agents. It was also vital that the Japanese did not learn of any success and increase their efforts.

Disappointed though they were at not going to war, the 555th set about the task of becoming the world's first Airborne fire-fighters with great professionalism. From Pendleton four officers and 96 troopers were also detached to Chico, California, and the jumps commenced.

Specialised equipment was needed, for jumping into trees is dangerous and something most parachutists try to avoid. Modified baseball helmets with mesh face-guards became de rigeur as did initially a 50ft rope to allow the trooper a descent from the treetops. Over their standard fatigues the men also wore Air Force fleece-lined flying jackets and trousers, the tough leather giving additional protection.

Whilst there were the usual injuries through jumping (including one man who suffered a spinal injury and walked 18 miles to the airstrip for pick up rather than burden his colleagues) the only fatality the unit suffered in 1,236 jumps was a trooper who fell to his death after running out of rope when jumping into giant redwoods Following this incident a 150ft rope became standard issue.

The 555th also used a modified

Below: The 'Triple Nickles', the 555th Parachute Infantry Battalion. (US Army)

'chute, known as the 'Derry', with one panel missing which allowed more manoeuvrability than the standard model. This of course presaged modern 'chutes which can be steered with some precision.

The tree jumping continued from May to August 1945, following which the Nickles returned to Fort Bragg where they were initially attached to 27th Headquarters and Headquarters Special Troops First Army. In December they were attached to the 13th Airborne. Still retaining its own authority and discipline the 555th was in something of a limbo during this period as men began to receive their discharge papers and go home. Finally in February 1946 the Triple Nickles became a battalion attached for administrative purposes to the 504th. The 504th's colonel at the time was a man who was to rise to great prominence later—William Westmoreland. Gavin, who knew good soldiers when he saw them, made sure that the Triple Nickles were part of the victory parade as full members of the 82nd Airborne. The Army meanwhile was only slowly coming to recognise their worth.

What made the 555th unique amongst 'colored' units in US service was that it was the only formation which was all-black, officers and men (other units had black enlisted men and white officers). The troopers had also had to deal with the ignorance and bigotry of the time throughout their existence. This they accomplished with the professionalism, self-confidence and pride that comes with being Airborne. Whatever ill-informed society thought, these men knew they were the best of the best. So well did they acquit themselves in fact that in 1947 Gavin went personally to Washington to request that they become a permanent part of the 82nd. This far-sighted move was made at some professional risk—there remains a feeling in some quarters that Gavin retired without a fourth star because of his support for the 555th.

On 13 December 1947 the 555th was de-activated, its colours cased, and it became the 3rd Battalion, 505th. History was not done with the Nickles yet. In July 1948 President Truman ordered that the US forces be integrated and in December the 3rd/505th was de-activated and its personnel absorbed into the 82nd as a whole. The process of integration was greatly aided by the officers and men of the unit who gradually took their professionalism out into the wider Army community as they dispersed on different assignments.

More than one member of the 82nd has commented to this author that much of the heartache and racial tension of the fifties and sixties would have been avoided if men of all races had served together in WWII. Bonds and mutual respect forged in the crucible of war are not easily broken—'there are', as one veteran said, 'no racial or religious differences in a fox hole.'

The modern US Army owes a considerable debt to the 555th, a debt most recently acknowledged by no lesser person than Colin Powell, America's most senior black soldier. He credits the 555th with setting the stage that enabled his rise to the very top of his profession.

Many of the original members of the 555th went on to achieve high rank and do great things in the post-war Army. One of the original platoon members, Sergeant Roger S. Walden won a Silver Star in Korea for instance. Today, wherever the veterans go, young paratroopers want to shake their hands—one ex-trooper, Cecil Malone, still jumps, drawing thunderous applause as he executes perfect landings in front of three generations of paratroopers. The Nickles will not be forgotten, or for that matter fade away.

Below: The US flag goes up over a town in East Germany during the final days of the European campaign. During three years of war 82nd had notched up 422 days in combat. Over 3,200 personnel had been killed in action out of a total missing, wounded, injured or killed of over 15,000—more than the strength of a complete late 1944 division, approximately 13,000 men. (82nd Airborne Museum)

PARATROOP RIFLE COMPANY AIRCRAFT LOADING FOR MARKET GARDEN

AIRCRAFT #1—15 men,
2 containers

Company CO
2 x Radio operators
2 x Messengers
2 x ATRL squads (gunner
  and asst gunner)
2 x Riflemen
Armorer artificer
QM sergeant
Cargo sergeant
1st sergeant

A5 CONTAINER # 1
2 x ATRLs in frame
4 x bags ammo (ea 6 rockets)
2 x blankets

A5 CONTAINER # 2
1 x Gas alarm
1 x SCR 300 radio
1 x SCR battery
1 x Panel, AP50A, set
1 x EE8A
2 x blankets and 2 x 2 by 4s

AIRCRAFT #3—19 men,
3 containers
2nd Squad 1st Platoon

Platoon sergeant
1 x LMG squad (gunner, asst
  gunner, ammo bearer)
AT grenadier
1 x Rifle squad (leader, asst
  leader, 6 x riflemen)
1 x Mortar squad (leader,
  gunner, asst gunner)
3 x Ammo bearers

A5 CONTAINER # 5
1 x 60mm mortar
4 x ammo vests (ea 10 rounds)
1 x camo net
2 x 2 by 4s
2 x blankets

A5 CONTAINER # 6
1 x LMG and spare barrel
1 x pair shoulder pads
4 x boxes MG ammo
1 x camo net
2 x ammo bags (ea 5 AT gren)

A5 CONTAINER # 7
7 x boxes MG ammo
20 rounds 60mm ammo
2 x blankets and 2 x 2 by 4s

AIRCRAFT #5—16 men,
2 containers
1st Squad 2nd Platoon

2nd Platoon leader
Radio operator
1 x LMG squad (gunner, asst
  gunner, ammo bearer)
AT grenadier
Aid man
Messenger
1 x Rifle squad (leader, asst
  leader, 6 x riflemen)

A5 CONTAINER # 10
1 x LMG and spare barrel
1 x pair shoulder pads
4 x boxes MG ammo
1 x camo net
2 x ammo bags (ea 5 AT gren)
2 x blankets

A5 CONTAINER # 11
7 x boxes MG ammo
20 rounds 60mm ammo
2 x blankets and 2 x 2 by 4s

AIRCRAFT #7—15 men,
2 containers
3rd Squad 2nd Platoon

2nd Platoon assistant leader
Messenger
1 x LMG squad (gunner, asst
  gunner, ammo bearer)
AT grenadier
1 x Rifle squad (leader, asst
  leader, 6 x riflemen)
Signal corpsman

A5 CONTAINER # 15
1 x LMG and spare barrel
1 x pair shoulder pads
4 x boxes MG ammo
1 x camo net
2 x ammo bags (ea 5 AT gren)

A5 CONTAINER # 16
7 x boxes MG ammo
20 rounds 60mm ammo
2 x blankets and 2 x 2 by 4s

AIRCRAFT #9—19 men,
3 containers
2nd Squad 3rd Platoon

Platoon sergeant
1 x LMG squad (gunner, asst
  gunner, ammo bearer)
AT grenadier
1 x Rifle squad (leader, asst
  leader, 6 x riflemen)
1 x Mortar squad (leader,
  gunner, asst gunner)
3 x Ammo bearers

A5 CONTAINER # 19
1 x 60mm mortar
4 x ammo vests (ea 10 rounds)
1 x camo net
2 x 2 by 4s
2 x blankets

A5 CONTAINER # 20
1 x LMG and spare barrel
1 x pair shoulder pads
4 x boxes MG ammo
1 x camo net
2 x ammo bags (ea 5 AT gren)

A5 CONTAINER # 21
7 x boxes MG ammo
20 rounds 60mm ammo
2 x blankets and 2 x 2 by 4s

AIRCRAFT #11—15 men,
2 containers

Company executive officer
Radio operator (300 set)
Messenger
2 x ATRL squads (gunner
  and asst gunner)
4 x Riflemen

A5 CONTAINER # 24 AND # 25
2 x ATRLs in frame
4 x bags ammo (ea 6 rockets)
2 x blankets

Eleven aircraft were needed to carry a paratroop
rifle company during Operation Market Garden,
loaded as shown here. On D-Day, 17 September
1944, 413 C-47s and C-53s carried 6,312
paratroops to the dropzone.

AIRCRAFT #6—19 men,
3 containers
2nd Squad 2nd Platoon

Platoon sergeant
1 x LMG squad (gunner, asst
  gunner, ammo bearer)
AT grenadier
1 x Rifle squad (leader, asst
  leader, 6 x riflemen)
1 x Mortar squad (leader,
  gunner, asst gunner)
3 x Ammo bearer

A5 CONTAINER # 12
1 x 60mm mortar
4 x ammo vests (ea 10 rounds)
1 x camo net
2 x blankets and 2 x 2 by 4s

A5 CONTAINER # 13
1 x LMG and spare barrel
1 x pair shoulder pads
4 x boxes MG ammo
1 x camo net
2 x ammo bags (ea 5 AT gren)

A5 CONTAINER # 14
7 x boxes MG ammo
20 rounds 60mm ammo
2 x blankets and 2 x 2 by 4s

AIRCRAFT # 2—16 men,
2 containers
1st Squad 1st Platoon

1st Platoon leader
Radio operator
1 x LMG squad (gunner, asst
  gunner, ammo bearer)
AT grenadier
Aid man
Messenger
1 x Rifle squad (leader, asst
  leader, 6 x riflemen)

A5 CONTAINER # 3
1 x LMG and spare barrel
1 x pair shoulder pads
4 x boxes MG ammo
1 x camo net
2 x ammo bags (ea 5 AT gren)
2 x blankets

A5 CONTAINER # 4
7 x boxes MG ammo
20 rounds 60mm ammo
2 x blankets and 2 x 2 by 4s

AIRCRAFT #4—15 men,
2 containers
3rd Squad 1st Platoon

1st Platoon assistant leader
Messenger
1 x LMG squad (gunner, asst
  gunner, ammo bearer)
AT grenadier
1 x Rifle squad (leader, asst
  leader, 6 x riflemen)
Signal corpsman

A5 CONTAINER # 8
1 x LMG and spare barrel
1 x pair shoulder pads
4 x boxes MG ammo
1 x camo net
2 x ammo bags (ea 5 AT gren)

A5 CONTAINER # 9
7 x boxes MG ammo
20 rounds 60mm ammo
2 x blankets and 2 x 2 by 4s

AIRCRAFT #8—16 men,
2 containers
1st Squad 3rd Platoon

3rd Platoon leader
Radio operator
1 x LMG squad (gunner, asst
  gunner, ammo bearer)
AT grenadier
Aid man
Messenger
1 x Rifle squad (leader, asst
  leader, 6 x riflemen)

A5 CONTAINER # 17
1 x LMG and spare barrel
1 x pair shoulder pads
4 x boxes MG ammo
1 x camo net
2 x ammo bags (ea 5 AT gren)
2 x blankets

A5 CONTAINER # 18
7 x boxes MG ammo
20 rounds 60mm ammo
2 x blankets and 2 x 2 by 4s

AIRCRAFT #10—15 men,
2 containers
3rd Squad 3rd Platoon

3rd Platoon assistant leader
Messenger
1 x LMG squad (gunner, asst
  gunner, ammo bearer)
AT grenadier
1 x Rifle squad (leader, asst
  leader, 6 x riflemen)
Signal corpsman

A5 CONTAINER # 22
1 x LMG and spare barrel
1 x pair shoulder pads
4 x boxes MG ammo
1 x camo net
2 x ammo bags (ea 5 AT gren)

A5 CONTAINER # 23
7 x boxes MG ammo
20 rounds 60mm ammo
2 x blankets and 2 x 2 by 4

82nd AIRBORNE DIVISION as at the Battle of the Bulge

Division HQ —— HQ Company

EQUIPMENT & MARKINGS

EQUIPMENT

No analysis of the 82nd in World War II would be complete without some discussion of its equipment, particularly the aircraft, gliders and parachutes that gave the Airborne its special capabilities.

Douglas C-47 Dakota
The Dakota, developed from the civil DC-3, was so successful that it quickly became the backbone of Allied air transport operations, British and American. Capable of lifting cargo or troops, and towing gliders it quickly replaced the motley collection of aircraft (usually converted obsolete bombers) used by the British Airborne for dropping paratroops. Post-war demobbed C-47s formed the core of many a nascent airline, and considerable numbers fly to this day.

Capacity: 3 crew + 24 paratroopers
Span: 95ft 6in
Length: 63ft 9in
Weight, empty: 17,700lb
Weight, loaded: 26,000lb
Cruising speed: 160mph
Top speed: 230mph
Ceiling: 24,000ft

Curtiss C-46 Commando
Designed to do the same job as the Dakota, the C-46 had a much greater capacity (in both weight and volume) and featured doors on both sides of the fuselage to allow more efficient dispatch of troops. The aircraft was trialled during the Arnhem operation but suffered high losses with an apparent tendency to burst into flame rather easily. It was not used in the European theatre after that.

Capacity: 3 crew + 40 paratroopers
Span: 108ft
Length: 76ft 4in
Weight, empty: 29,300lb
Weight, loaded: 50,000lb
Cruising speed: 235mph
Top speed: 270mph
Ceiling: 22,000ft

Above right: C-47 showing under-fuselage equipment container stowage. (See page 66 for contents of these.) The unusual combination of British and United States' national markings in this wartime photograph suggest that the aircraft is flying over North Africa in 1943. (Museum of Army Flying)

Below right: Preserved C-47 with invasion stripes outside the Airborne Museum at Fort Bragg. Behind is a C-46—used briefly in Europe, it proved unsuitable and was relegated to the Far East. Another excellent C-47 can be seen at the new museum in Ste-Mère-Église. (Mike Verier)

This sequence of photos (see also pages 74–75) is obviously posed. Its quality, however, is so good that the pictures might have been taken yesterday. They represent a unique colour record of Airborne uniforms and equipment just before the Sicily landings.

Far left and Below: Paratroopers 'chuting up with T5 parachutes. Note the paratrooper boots and cumbersome entrenching tool. The trooper nearest the camera is just attaching his reserve to the harness. (US Army via 82nd Division Museum)

Left: This next soldier is wearing a parachute but interestingly seems to have a standard M1 'infantry' helmet. The Flag patch is worn on the left shoulder— the right was more common—and prominent on the left thigh is the canvas gasmask cover. (US Army via 82nd Division Museum)

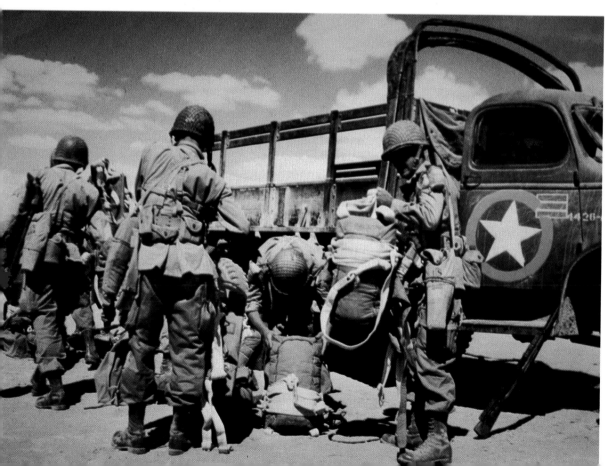

Waco CG-4A

The most numerous of the Allied types, the CG-4 was a workmanlike machine of welded tube and fabric construction. The nose section was hinged upwards to permit unrestricted access to the essentially square-section fuselage capable of accommodating a jeep or artillery piece. In British service it was named Hadrian, a sobriquet not apparently used by the Americans.

Capacity: 2 crew + 13/15 soldiers (or 1 jeep/artillery piece and 6 soldiers)
Span: 83ft 6in
Length: 48ft
Weight, empty: 3,400lb
Weight, loaded: 7,500lb

Airspeed AS 51/AS 58 Horsa

Whilst a competent enough aircraft, the Horsa was constructed entirely of wood and roundly disliked by British and American troopers alike because of the way it would splinter in the barely controlled crash that a combat landing so often became. It was capable of accepting a jeep or similar. Two variants were built, the slightly larger Mark II having a hinged nose making access to the load more straightforward—the Mk I's tail had to be removed after landing. It was built (often in sub-assemblies by furniture factories) in large numbers and saw service on most Allied operations

Capacity: 2 crew + 25 soldiers
Span: 110ft
Length: 67ft (Mark I); 67ft 11in (Mark II)
Weight, empty: 8,370lb
Weight, loaded: 15,500lb (Mark I); 15,750lb (Mark II)

Above: Landing a glider was never straightforward—indeed, most of the time it was particularly dangerous. The risks were not restricted to enemy gunfire or uneven landing grounds, some crews were killed by their own loads breaking loose and crushing them. This casualty is a Waco CG-4A. (Museum of Army Flying)

Below: A British Horsa takes-off for Normandy towed by a Halifax. Note the twin tow attachments under the glider's wings. (Museum of Army Flying)

Above: View of General Aircraft Ltd's factory showing the prototype Hamilcar and, in front, the production line of the smaller Hotspur. Designed along the same lines as the German DFS 230, it was relegated to a training role by the much bigger Horsa. (Museum of Army Flying)

Left: Waco CG-4 gliders collected together for return to the UK following landings during the Dutch campaign. More survived the daylight landings here, when compared with the vast numbers written off during the Normandy operations. (via Bruce Robertson)

General Aircraft GAL 49 Hamilcar

The largest glider built by the Allies, the Hamilcar was designed to bring heavy loads and vehicles to the battlefield. The cockpit sat above a 'straight through' cabin accessed via a hinged nose. The Hamilcar had the distinction of a tank (the Tetrarch) specially designed to fit in it. A powered version was trialled, but the war ended before it could be put in service.

Capacity: 1 x Tetrach or Locust; or 2 x Bren carrriers; or bulldozer
Span: 110ft
Length: 68ft
Weight, loaded: 32,500lb

Below: Study of a General Aircraft Hamilcar. The last remaining Hamilcar fuselage—discovered performing as a garden shed—is on show at Middle Wallop. (Museum of Army Flying)

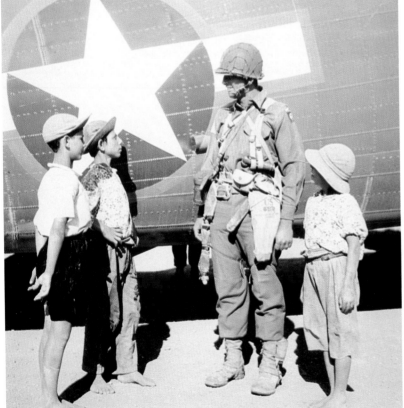

Above: Officers at a briefing. Note the variety of shirt colours and the inconsistent placing of the 82nd Division patch. The man with his back to the camera wears American belt equipment (including, presumably, the .45 automatic behind him) but the beret suggests he may be French. (US Army via 82nd Division Museum)

Left: Despite the C-47 in the background (note red outline to National insignia confirming date as 1943), this lieutenant is a gliderman as evidenced by his infantry leggings. He has a field dressing taped to his left leg and carries binoculars in a brown leather case, as well as the ubiquitous right-angle torch. The large pouch at his thigh is for a gas mask and bears the markings of the Chemical Corps under the 'US'. The 82nd Division patch is worn on his left shoulder and the Stars and Stripes patch can just be made out on the other arm. He is to be wearing the M1C airborne helmet. (US Army via 82nd Division Museum)

Right: Fully rigged paratroopers by the door of a C-47. The aft door was for bulky items of freight (in the freighter role the Dakota could carry a jeep) For dropping paratroops, however, this door was not used. Two crewmen are taping over the handle to ensure there is nothing to foul the jumpers' harnesses or static lines. (US Army via 82nd Division Museum)

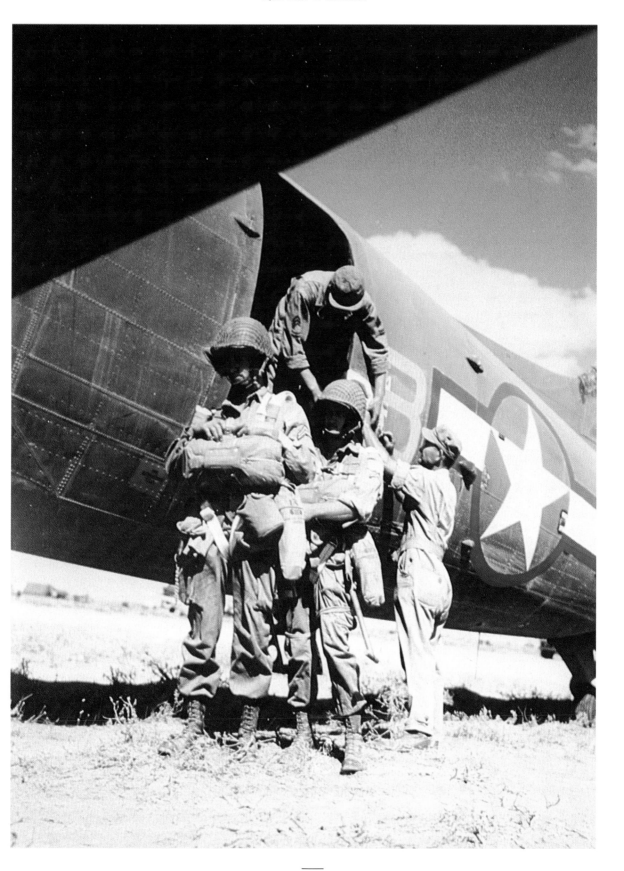

Part of the Presidential Unit Citation of Company A, 504th PIR for crossing Rhine River at Hitdorf, Germany on 6 April 1945.

Company A . . . is cited for outstanding performance of duty in the armed conflict against the enemy . . . This company crossed the Rhine River at 02:30 hours 6 April 1945, and seized the mile-long town of Hitdorf on the east shore with the mission of providing a base for further patrolling and to cause the German High Command to commit disproportionate forces against them in the belief that it was to be a major river crossing . . . the Germans assembled and directed a considerable portion of two divisions to the mission of containing and annihilating the . . . [US forces]. In mid-afternoon the entire area was subjected to a withering and devastating artillery barrage for two hours, after which counter-attacking forces in overwhelming strength with tank support assaulted the defending troopers from every direction . . . The troopers of Company A doggedly stood their ground, fought at close quarters, and at point blank range and inflicted terrible casualties on the masses of the enemy. Fighting with relentless ferocity throughout the afternoon and night, this gallant company held its ground and carried out its mission until it was finally ordered to withdraw to the west bank of the Rhine on the night of 6-7 April . . . Eighty prisoners were taken and evacuated and conservative estimates indicate that 150 of the enemy were killed and 250 wounded. The conduct of Company A reflects great credit on the Airborne Forces of the United States Army.

Parachutes

The three major airborne forces of WWII used 'chutes that were superficially similar in that they all had 28ft diameter canopies. In their detail operation they were quite different however.

The US Airborne's first attempt was the T4. A workmanlike job, the rig featured a reserve (emergency) 'chute which was carried vertically on the trooper's chest leaving little room for other equipment. Like all the parachutes for assault troops, it relied on a static line to open the main canopy once the soldier dropped clear of the aircraft (the reserve of course was manually operated). The T4 was superseded by the T5 by the time of the first operational jumps. The principal observable difference was the horizontal stowage of the reserve 'chute. (The Americans were the only combatants to use a reserve. With typical British phlegm their decision not to was originally based on the small size of the 'hole in the floor' exit on a Whitley, and later on cost. The Germans jumped from much lower altitude with a rig that in any case made a reserve impracticable.)

Both the American designs suffered from not having a single point quick-release (it was felt that troopers might fall out of the harness too easily). This, however, meant that getting out of the harness on the ground could be a struggle, taking up precious seconds and making the trooper vulnerable. This latter point was addressed by the T7 (first issued in 1944) which did have a quick-release.

A more serious complaint was that all three US parachutes had the canopy opening first, before all the rigging deployed. This resulted in the wearer going from 120mph to almost zero in a few feet as the canopy 'stopped' to deploy whilst the shroud lines paid out and then snapped the falling trooper to a halt. Such was the violence of this arrested motion that in Normandy some troopers found that grenades in their pockets simply burst through the seams and were lost.

The Germans also had a 'canopy first' 'chute, the RZ 20, which was even more demanding of the trooper. Unlike the British and American rigs in which the canopy lines were gathered into four risers, the Germans had a single point suspension which met an inverted V-strop attached to rings either side of the jumper's waist (inexplicably, as their standard aircrew parachutes were entirely conventional). This meant that the *Fallschirmjäger* had no control over direction or rate of descent. Worse, when the canopy snapped open he would jacknife due to being suspended from the waist. This arrangement resulted in a 'face forward' landing attitude. The one tactical advantage of the RZ 20 was its ability to cope with very low altitude drops. In Crete some sticks went out as low as 250 feet.

The British X-Type parachute on the other hand had none of the vices suffered by its contemporaries. Like the American T-Series it had four risers and the incumbent rode down in an almost sitting posture. Like the American rig the ability to 'spill' air from the canopy by pulling on the risers gave a measure of control, enabling the jumper to turn into wind for landing and to a certain extent steer away from obstacles (not that there was much time for such niceties at 500 feet in the dark). The X-Type also featured the classic 'turn and strike' quick-release, which made getting out of the harness a simple operation, saving vital seconds after landing.

Its most important feature, unlike the others, was a 'canopy last' deployment. Essentially the static line pulled the canopy out of the pack in a bag or sheath. The shroud lines then paid out evenly until they pulled the canopy out of its bag. The deceleration for the paratrooper was thus more even as the canopy developed. The downside was that it was therefore slower-opening than the German or American models, and less able to cope with low altitude drops. It was nevertheless acknowledged as the most reliable of all the parachutes used during the conflict.

Above: King George VI inspects British Paras wearing X-Type parachutes. (via Mike Verier)

Left: In full flight under his RZ 20, a Fallschirmjäger had no control over his descent because of the single point harness and bacause the shroud lines were too high above his head to be reached—well illustrated despite the poor quality of this photograph. (via Chris Ellis)

Left: 82nd Airborne re-enactor in full equipment—T5 parachute (the white of the static line that operates it just visible) on his back; reserve 'chute with red ripcord handle on his front; full belt, webbing, canteen, pistol, entrenching tool and knife; life vest; pack hanging between his legs; Griswold bag (on his right side and only visible under his right knee) containing his rifle; compass attached to shoulder strap; black waterproof bag (on left thigh) containing gasmask; Hawkins mine (the brown can on his left ankle); AN/PPN-2 transmitter/receiver beacon (in canvas bag in his left hand); unlined horsehide riding gloves; and, of course, M1C helmet and field dressing. (Tim Hawkins)

Right: Another re-enactment photograph showing a well-laden paratrooper (but not fully laden! In combat every pocket would bulge with grenades, K-rations and field dressings). Apart from the kit outlined above, this man carries a Thompson M1 sub-machine gun, a TL122C right-angle flashlight; and an ammunition pouch for the M3 (on his right hip). Note the white rope skein and the bottom of his pistol and knife holsters. (Tim Hawkins)

PEOPLE

Above: Pike.

Above right: de Glopper.

Below right: Towle.

Below: York

MEDAL OF HONOR WINNERS

Lieutenant Colonel Emory J. Pike

From Columbia City, Iowa, Pike was Division Machine Gun Officer and won his medal for action near Vandieras, France, 15 September 1918. While on a front line reconnaissance mission, heavy artillery shelling disorganised advancing infantry units of the 325th. He re-organised the men, secured the position against attack, and went to the aid of a wounded soldier in an outpost, before being severely wounded by shell fire. He later died from these wounds.

Corporal Alvin C. York

From Fentress County, Tennessee, York was in Company G, 328th Infantry, and won his medal for action near Châtel-Chehery, France, 8 October 1918. Corporal, later Sergeant, York is one of the truly great names in American military history. His story is all the more remarkable that he was originally a conscientious objector who only agreed to volunteer for combat after much soul-searching.

As ever in the fortunes of war, York's platoon just happened to draw the assignment of silencing some machine guns. Frontal assault had failed and the four NCOs and thirteen privates were to attempt to steal up unobserved. York, a Tennessee woodsman, had the point and led the patrol so skillfully that they completely surprised some 75 Germans. York was forced to shoot one who resisted upon which the rest surrendered.

At this point other German machine guns opened up on the Americans killing nine, including the other three NCOs. Whilst the remaining seven soldiers took cover and tried to guard the prisoners, York calmly took his rifle and began picking off the MG crews with precisely aimed shots. The 1917 Enfield rifle only had a five round magazine, and realising this a German lieutenant led five men in a charge on York's position.

They had clearly never encountered someone who had grown up hunting turkeys in the Tennessee hills. York made every round count, and as the last man got close calmly drew his pistol (the famed .45 automatic, not a weapon noted for its accuracy) and dispatched him, too. Eventually, after some 25 Germans had been killed, the cowed survivors surrendered. York and his remaining soldiers rounded them up and marched them back, even acquiring one or two others en route. When they finally reached the battalion lines they had no fewer than 132 Germans including four officers, along with the captured Maxims.

York's exploits were immortalised by Gary Cooper in the Hollywood film *Sergeant York* (xxx).

Private First Class Charles N. de Glopper

From Grand Island, New York, de Glopper was serving in Company C, 325th Glider Infantry Regiment, when he won his medal for an action on 9 June 1944, at La Fière, France, on the Merderet River. Part of a platoon that had penetrated the German lines but found itself in danger of being completely cut off, de Glopper and his comrades were pinned down in a ditch. Seeing that the only way for them to withdraw was to provide covering fire, de Glopper stepped out onto the road with his BAR and began firing on the German positions.

He immediately drew a large volume of rifle and automatic fire but, although severely wounded, continued to return fire. Falling to his knees he still continued to fire burst after burst at the German positions until he was finally killed.

Through his sacrifice his fellow troopers had been able to get to a more secure position and continued the fight, securing the bridgehead. Afterwards many wrecked machine guns and dead Germans were found to attest to the effectiveness of his fire.

Private John R Towle

Of Cleveland, Ohio, Towle served in Company C, 504th Parachute Infantry Regiment. He won his medal in action near Oosterhout, Holland, 21 September 1944, during the Nijmegen action. Armed with a rocket launcher, Towle single-handedly, and without orders moved into an exposed position and broke up a German counter-attack against the recently taken bridge, driving off some 100 infantrymen supported by two tanks and a half track. He then turned his bazooka on a house being used as a strong point and destroyed that before he was mortally wounded by a mortar shell.

First Sergeant Leonard Funk Jr.

Funk came from Braddock Township, Pennsylvania, and was in Company C, 508th Parachute Infantry Regiment when he won his medal, in action at Holzheim, Belgium, 29 January 1945. Funk, a small unassuming man, probably ranks as the 82nd's greatest hero, since he won every major decoration it was possible to win, culminating in the Congressional Medal of Honor at Holzheim.

Funk was one of many troopers scattered in the Normandy drop. Despite a badly sprained ankle he eventually rounded up a group of 18 men and set out to regain friendly lines some 20 miles distant across hostile territory swarming with German troops. After three men at the point had been lost Sergeant Funk himself took the lead rather than jeopardise any more of his men. He

Above: Funk about to undertake a jump complete with dog 'Shorty'—the original note on the back of the photo (in his own handwriting) attributes the location as 'somewhere in France' and the date as April 1945.

Below: 20 January 1945. During a lull in the fighting men of the 82nd receive the Distinguished Service Cross for the action at Nijmegen the previous September. Left to right: Col Rueben H. Tucker, Lt-Col J. A. Cook, Capt. Wesley D. Harris, Lt John L. Foley, 1-Lt Lloyd L. Polette and S/Sgt. Shelton W. Dustin. (US Army)

continued to scout ahead of the group for the remainder of the journey, moving mainly at night. Finally after numerous encounters with enemy groups, he led his men through the German lines to regain his own side. This feat won him the Silver Star.

During the Nijmegen operations in September he led a three-man patrol against a German 20mm flak battery firing on gliders attempting to land. He drove off the defenders of the guns before leading an assault that killed 20 crew members and wounded many more. The guns were out of action before they could come to bear on the gliders. The Army awarded him the Distinguished Service Cross for 'courageous and heroic action'.

Finally he was involved in an incident during the Battle of the Bulge which was more than any other to demonstrate his fighting spirit. A group of around 80 German prisoners was being escorted to the rear when the few guards were approached by four 'troopers' in snow suits. At least one of their number was English speaking and the prisoners were duly left in their care whilst the original escort hastened to rejoin their unit.

As it transpired the 'troopers' were German paras who began to re-arm the others with the intention of attacking their erstwhile captors. At this point Sergeant Funk came upon the scene together with some other troopers. Once again the similarity of both sides' snow suits aided the Germans who used the resulting few seconds' hesitation to close on the Americans. Sergeant Funk suddenly found a machine pistol pressed into his ribs by the triumphant German officer who ordered him to surrender.

Funk, whose Thompson was slung barrel-up at his shoulder, stepped back and made as if to comply. Then with one swift movement and a shout of 'surrender hell!' swung the gun into his hand and riddled the German. Still standing in the middle of the road he then led the brief fire-fight that erupted, dispatching the others and regaining control of the situation.

Sergeant Funk survived the war to be presented with his Medal of Honor by President Truman in person, a truly remarkable soldier, even by the standards of the 82nd.

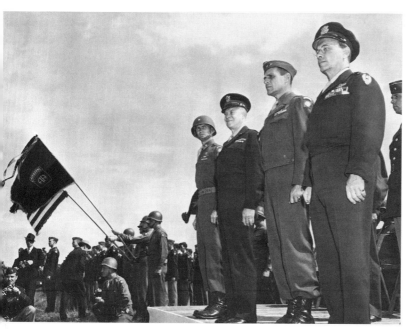

Left: 10 August 1944. This Change-of-Command Review in England was the occasion Ike made his 'I owe you a lot' address. A beaming Eisenhower is flanked by Gavin (with his trademark Airborne helmet) and Ridgway. Nearest the camera is Louis Brereton, who planned the D-Day drops. (US Army)

COMMANDING OFFICERS

World War I

Major General Eben Swift	25 August 1917 to 23 November 1917
Brigadier General James Erwin	24 November 1917 to 16 December 1917
Brigadier General William P. Burnham	27 December 1917 to 3 October 1918
Major General George B. Duncan	4 October 1918 to 21 May 1919

World War II

Major General Omar N. Bradley	23 March 1942 to 25 June 1942
Major General Mathew B. Ridgeway	26 June 1942 to 27 August 1944
Major General James M. Gavin	28 August 1944 to 26 March 1948

Major General Omar N. Bradley

Whilst Bradley only commanded the 82nd for a few months before going on to greater things, it was he who set it on the road to greatness. Had he not been so determined to get the division to a high standard it might not have become the nucleus of the Airborne. Bradley's deputy, Ridgway, proved to be an inspired choice, demonstrating that an élite formation will attract the best officers and soldiers. Both officers believed in not asking soldiers to do anything they would not do themselves and were to be seen on the assault course to prove it. Once in Europe the division had in Bradley an officer in the high command who recognised its capabilities and championed its cause. His influence on the 82nd was felt long after he had relinquished direct command.

Major General Matthew B. Ridgway

Matthew Ridgway was born on 3 March 1895 and graduated from the US Military Academy in 1917. After varied assignments and study in the service schools, he went to the Philippines, where he served as Technical Advisor to the Governor General in 1932–33. In the next few years he served in various staff posts and studied at the Army's Command and General Staff school and the War College.

In September 1939 Major Ridgway joined the War Plans Division in the War Department General Staff. Ridgway became Assistant Division Commander of the 82nd when the 82nd Infantry Division was reactivated on 25 March 1942 at Camp Claiborne, Louisiana. He succeeded to the command on 26 June 1942.

Under the wise leadership and skillful handling of its new commander, the 82nd soon developed into the most promising among the new units being quickly whipped into shape. On 15 August its designation was changed to 82nd Airborne Division, Major General Ridgway commanding. Half of its strength was subtracted to form the 101st Airborne Division. Ground training in new techniques commenced at Camp Claiborne. In early October the division had a foretaste of the future by shifting to Fort Bragg in the largest airborne troop movement ever attempted by the Army. Advanced ground training in alternation with flight exercises by both troop transport and parachute and by troop transport and gliders was pushed rigorously.

In the short space of eight months Major General Ridgway changed the 82nd from a brave dream into a deadly fighting machine. This amazing transformation was due entirely to the imagination, initiative and will power of a leader who was resolved that his command should become the premier airborne division of the Army, the first overseas and the first into battle. On 20 April 1943, the troopers left Fort Bragg en route for the combat zone.

In July 1943 the first major use of the Airborne was nearly a disaster, The destiny of the Airborne hung in the balance for many weeks thereafter until General Ridgway's convictions prevailed. Then General Clark called for help at Salerno. Eight hours later General Ridgway's troopers were on the DZ, and there was no doubting the value of the Airborne after that.

Ridgeway led the 82nd through the greatest invasion in history at Normandy. His planning and leadership resulted in the success of his division in that campaign despite the terrible losses it suffered during the initial drop. It was at this point with the Germans 400 yards from his CP, that he made his famous signal: 'Shor 60 percent infantry, 90 percent artillery, combat efficiency excellent.' The division fought on without relief for over a month in some of the war's hardest fighting, to take every objective assigned.

Following Normandy the division returned to the UK for re-fitting. In less than a month it was back to full strength and on 10 August 1944 Major General Ridgway assembled his reorganised division for a review by General Eisenhower. It was during this review that Eisenhower made his famous speech about how much he owed the 82nd.

Later that month, the XVIII Corps (Airborne) was born and General Ridgway became its commander, handing the command of the 82nd to Jim Gavin.

Major General James M. Gavin

'To the troopers of the 82d Airborne Division, who with courage and determination in their hearts, carried the fight to the enemy from Africa to Berlin. It has been a great privilege to have served in your ranks.' James M. Gavin.

Right: Major General M. D. Ridgway, CG XVIIIth Airborne Corps, and Major General J. H. Gavin (right), CG 82nd Airborne, talk somewhere in Belgium. Note Ridgway's trademark hand grenades and Gavin's 82nd Airborne Divisional patch. (via Real War Photos)

James M. Gavin was born in New York, New York, on 22 March 1907. At the age of seventeen, with some slight exaggeration about his age, he enlisted to begin career as one of the best military minds the US has ever produced. He served a private, private first class and corporal in the 16th and 2nd Coast Artiller

Above: Official portrait of Gavin. (82nd Airborne Museum)

Regiments in 1925 but his ambition was always to reach the US Military Academy, West Point. This he did, graduating from there with a Bachelor of Science degree and a commission as a 2nd Lieutenant, Infantry, on 13 June 1929.

In August 1941 Gavin attended the Parachute School and upon graduation was assigned to the 503rd Parachute Battalion. In December 1941 he was made Plans and Training Officer of the Provisional Parachute Group at Fort Benning, Georgia. In September 1942 he attended the Command and General Staff School at Fort Leavenworth, Kansas, and upon graduation was assigned to the Airborne Command at Fort Bragg, North Carolina, as G-3.

Gavin became Commanding Officer of the 505th Parachute Infantry in July 1942 and remained in that command when the regiment was assigned to the 82nd Airborne Division in January 1943. The 82nd Airborne Division went overseas in April and the 505th Parachute Combat Team under the command of Colonel Gavin spearheaded the assault of Sicily on the night of 9 July 1943. He commanded the regiment in the parachute landing at Salerno Bay on the night of 14 September 1943 and the following month was made Assistant Division Commander of the 82nd Airborne Division.

In November 1943 he was placed on Temporary Duty with COSSAC in England as Airborne Advisor to the Supreme Commander, remaining on that assignment until about 1 February 1944 when he returned to duty with the division which had now arrived at Leicester.

In the Normandy invasion on the night of 5/6 June 1944 he commanded the parachute assault echelon of the 82nd Airborne Division, consisting of the 505th 507th, and 508th Infantries. Upon being relieved from the Normandy front, the division returned to England in July 1944 and on 28 August General Gavin assumed command of the division, the youngest divisional general in the Army.

As division commander he led the division in the airborne operation at Nijmegen, in the Battle of the Bulge the following winter, and the spring offensive of 1945, until the surrender of the German Army. The division was assigned to duty in Berlin in July 1945 where Gavin served as American representative on the City Kommandantura until the division left that city in October 1945.

Known universally to his men as 'Slim Jim', Gavin was a natural leader, always first to jump. Dressed and armed exactly as they were, he led from the front. In

Holland he suffered cracked vertebrae during the jump (a terribly painful injury) and not once did it appear to slow him down. His chief of staff at the time, Colonel Weinecke once commented 'We have a wonderful system worked out, I stay home with the telephones, and my general goes out and fights with the troops.' His troops loved him, more so that he had a fine tactical mind which was able to apply fully the skills the Airborne possessed. The success of the 82nd owed more to Gavin than almost anything else.

Major General William C. Lee

Known with good reason as 'the Father of the Airborne' Bill Lee's career was cut short by a heart attack in February 1944. His contribution to the development of the Airborne, however, was immense.

Born in March 1895, Lee was commissioned into the US Army in the spring of 1917 as a 2nd lieutenant. He served some 18 months in Europe, first as an infantry platoon commander and then as company commander, rising to the rank of captain.

After the war he graduated from North Carolina State in 1920 and from the US Army's Officer School at Fort Benning in 1922. His various assignments between then and 1940 included observation of the burgeoning German airborne force. By now Major Lee, he returned to a staff job in Washington convinced that the US, too, should have paratroops. His enthusiasm and position earned him the command of the Test Platoon which so ably proved the concept of airborne soldiers.

By March 1941 Lee had been promoted to lieutenant colonel and was in command of the Provisional Parachute Group at Fort Benning and busily honing the skills and equipment an airborne force would need. As was to become essential for all Airborne officers Lee underwent the same training and jump qualifications as his men, despite being more than twice the age of the average trooper.

With the expansion of the Airborne came further responsibility and promotion. By mid 1942 Lee was a brigadier general in command of the Airborne Command Headquarters, re-located at Camp MacKall. With full activation of the Army's first airborne divisions in August 1942 came command of the 101st and the rank of major general.

Ironically, having built the Airborne from scratch, Bill Lee was denied the chance of leading his men into combat when, on 5 February 1944, his soldiers in England and ready to go, he suffered a heart attack. Invalided out of the Army in October that year he nevertheless continued to work for the Airborne, serving as the UN's first airborne advisor until his death in 1948.

Brigadier General William Yarborough

No look at the personalities of the 82nd would be complete without mention of Yarborough. One of the early pioneers, he contributed hugely to the Airborne. As a lieutenant in the 501st he designed the Airborne Brevet, the special uniforms with large cargo pockets, and most treasured of all, the Airborne jump boots.

By the time of Operation Husky he had risen to lieutenant colonel commanding the 2nd/ 504th. No mean soldier either, he and two troopers took over 100 Italian prisoners whilst supposedly on a recce mission during that operation. Later, as commander of the 509th, he instituted the wearing of small silver stars to indicate combat jumps, a practice taken up throughout the Airborne.

Postwar his interest in uniform and equipment continued, in the sixties as a brigadier general he was instrumental in the adoption of the green beret by Special Forces. He was also involved in designing jungle clothing suitable for South-East Asia.

Above: The 'Father of Airborne' has his own museum in his home at Dunn, NC.

POSTWAR

The first post-war task the 82nd faced, even as its Honor Guard impressed the great and the good who visited Berlin, was to stay in existence. With officialdom's usual disregard for military achievement once a war is over, the 82nd was due for disbandment. Gavin used the opportunity presented by the hordes of important visitors to lobby for a permanent place in the Army's plans for the future.

During its time in Berlin the division received many honours, the most famous and unique of these being two presented to the entire division by grateful countries it had been instrumental in liberating. By royal order the Belgian Minister of National Defence presented the Belgian Fourragère to the division whilst the Dutch granted the 82nd the Willems-Orde orange lanyard. Soldiers of the division wear both decorations with pride to this day.

The division had won much respect in high places and was kept alive as part of the strategic reserve, becoming part of the regular Army in 1948 and thus assuring its future. During this time, the new atomic era, much debate raged about how to use airborne forces. The positions ranged from 'do we need them at all?' all the way to 'train the whole Army to be airborne'. Gavin, as ever years ahead of his time, continued to be the principal advocate and theorist of airborne tactics and predicted most of the modern developments.

'Developments' is the appropriate word. Sound tactics remain just that, it is equipment that changes. Thus when Colonel Jay Vanderpool's men at Fort Rucker were developing 'Airmobile' forces in the late 1950s, the mobility offered by the helicopter was combined with tactics from an 1898 manual for horse soldiers!

The division therefore remained combat ready. Ironically its high state of training kept it out of the Korean War for fear of a Russian or Chinese attack elsewhere. This meant that less capable divisions went to Korea with a consequent lengthening of the conflict.

Through the 1950s the 82nd trained for any contingency. Although primarily expecting to fight in Europe, if anywhere, it trained for territories from the Arctic to the jungle. The equipment continued to improve. The gliders were gradually phased out as new aircraft

Below: President Harry S. Truman and Secretary of the Army Frank Pace Jr in the Rose Garden behind the White House with men of the 82nd Airborne Division who toured the capital in February 1951. (via Real War Photos)

such as the C-119 Boxcar were introduced. At the end of the decade the classic C-130 Hercules arrived and continues to serve in updated form to this day. At the height of the Cold War in 1962 came the Cuban Missile Crisis. The level of brinkmanship was such that the 82nd was actually 'chuted up and ready to drop at the point when the Soviets finally backed down.

There were a number of structural re-organisations during this period, but the division's first actual (non exercise) deployment since 1945 came in 1965 when the USA intervened in the Dominican Republic's civil war. Elements of the 82nd remained there for some 17 months.

By this time the USA was involved in Vietnam. Once more the 82nd was held in reserve but as protests about this unpopular war grew so did civil unrest and rioting on the streets of America. In 1967 it was decided to use the Airborne to restore law and order. This, of course, was a controversial decision—rather like the British use of paratroops in Northern Ireland it could have led to even greater provocation. In the American case, however, the reverse proved to be true. Thanks to the efforts of the 555th and Gavin's early foresight, the 82nd by now contained large numbers of black soldiers at all levels. Seeing these men patrolling the ghettos proudly wearing the uniform of the nation's finest division made it hard for those intent on fomenting trouble to claim racist oppression. It was not a duty the troopers relished but their discipline remained unshaken and they carried it out professionally.

Meanwhile the 3rd Brigade was rushed to Vietnam to counter the Tet Offensive in 1968. This left the division very thinly stretched indeed and a 4th Brigade was formed to bring it back to strength.

During the 1970s the 82nd continued to train. Maintaining the standards it strove for was difficult in the post-Vietnam era but the division, probably because of its élite status, suffered less than other parts of the Army. Two major alerts brought the division's ready elements to within hours of deployment during this period. May 1978 saw the 82nd preparing for a jump on Kolwezi in Zaire to rescue civilians. In the event political prevarication meant that the French Foreign Legion went instead. Their successful combat jump was, however, to provide a powerful illustration of what could be achieved.

In November 1979 the fall of the Shah of Iran and the seizure of hostages in Teheran again saw the 82nd ready to go. Again it was not deployed on political grounds. Fort Bragg, however, was more than somewhat involved in the failed rescue mission that was mounted. Debacle though it was, valuable lessons were learnt and changes made for the benefit of the Army in the long run.

A new decade saw the 82nd serving as peacekeepers in that most volatile part of the world the Gaza Strip. For six months in 1982 the troopers of the 82nd kept the peace and worked (fortuitously as it later turned out) on their desert training. The following year the Airborne teamed with the Marines to restore the rightful government in Grenada. Operation Urgent Fury saw the first combat use of the new Kevlar

Below: 82nd Airborne train for combat in Saudi Arabia during 'Desert Shield'. (82nd Airborne)

helmet, and the UH-60 Blackhawk helicopter which was just beginning to replace the ubiquitous UH-1 Huey.

In March 1988 following an incursion by Nicaragua, the 82nd was deployed to Honduras. The mere presence of the paras was sufficient to ensure withdrawal, nobody now doubting that they meant business. By this time the shape of the division had changed, too, with better aircraft and equipment now on line, and increasingly, a true night capability. This capability was tested in December 1989 when the 82nd was instrumental in Operation Just Cause, the arrest of General Noriega in Panama. Panama also saw the first combat deployment of the awesome AH-64 Apache second generation attack helicopter.

The 82nd's biggest deployment since WWII came when Saddam Hussein invaded Kuwait in August 1990. As ever the Airborne went first. The 3rd/504th was for some time the only real force the Alliance could muster in theatre, though the troopers considered it lucky for Saddam that he did not attack them. When the shooting did eventually start it was, unsurprisingly, the Airborne who went further into Iraq than any other American force.

Since Desert Storm the division has not been idle either. Members of the division help keep the peace in the Balkans, whilst the development of new equipment and the relentless training keep them at the cutting edge. Nowadays, too, women troopers jump alongside the men—whilst they are still excluded from front line combat, most other specialities within the Army are open to women. That means that there are plenty of them in the 82nd, and that in turn means they have to jump. When the 82nd goes everyone goes, from the CG to the lowliest private soldier.

In the post Cold War age of defence cuts and 'drawdown' there are once again voices questioning the validity of airborne troops. It is to be hoped that those who criticise realise that they are free to do so because airborne soldiers gave their lives defending that right.

Below: Another sign of the times—a woman MP of 82nd Airborne in Panama. Note the Blackhawk in the background and the .50 cal Browning in the front. (82nd Airborne)

ASSESSMENT

Any discussion of how a unit performed can easily get bogged down in statistics. Perhaps the most important one in this case is how many good men died to achieve what the Airborne did. A better measure, if it could be made, would be how many did not die because of what the 82nd achieved.

There is no question that Airborne forces shortened the war, and that they were unable to shorten it further due to the failure of Market Garden was not of their making.

Right from the first operations they proved effective far beyond the numbers committed. Kurt Student, founder of Germany's much vaunted *Fallschirmjäger*, stated that had not the 82nd prevented a Panzer division reaching the beaches, the Allies would have been repulsed from Sicily. The Normandy invasion for all the air and sea power, for all the men hurled ashore, could well have had a different outcome without the Airborne, and for all that is written about Arnhem the fact remains that Airborne forces caused the Germans irreparable attrition. In the Ardennes, amidst indescribable conditions and having been caught by surprise, the Airborne took on and defeated the finest divisions the Germans had, preventing Hitler from splitting the Allies both politically and militarily.

In this last campaign of course they fought as infantry, without using their special Airborne capabilities—they just happened to be the available reserve. The point of course is that, unlike almost any other formation that could have been there, they were the ones with the skill, the determination, the tenacity and the confidence that being part of the Airborne had given them. Compared to 'ordinary' infantry Airborne soldiers were more motivated, better trained and better led. It is those three qualities that mark out élite units.

The men of the Airborne also built something this author has only come across in one other formation in the US military. Those who have served in the armed forces mostly speak generically about being 'in the Navy 'or 'in the Air Force'. The bonds formed in close knit élite forces, however, remain for life. In much the same way that anyone who has served in the USMC 'is a Marine' so the 82nd's veterans are 'Airborne'. This ésprit de corps extends across generations and remains as strong today as ever. That is a good sign for a society in an age of increasing selfishness and insecurity.

Above: After the problems of Sicily, US airborne troops—and 82nd in particular—performed with great skill and tenacity in attack and defence. Here, men of the 1st Battalion, 505th Regiment track down the enemy in winter conditions, January 1945. (via Real War photos)

Right: There are many memorials to the 82nd Airborne Division, such as the famous obelisk at Fort Bragg. This is the Memorial to the US Army Parachute Test Platoon—'We led the way'—at the Airborne and Special Operations Museum, Fayetteville. (Mike Verier)

Below and Below left: The original 'Iron Mike' Memorial is the work of Leah Herbert—he now has a replica at the La Fière bridge in France. (Mike Verier)

Below centre: Airborne memorial at Grave bridge. (Mike Verier)

Below right: Exhibit in the Ste-Mère-Église Airborne Museum commemorating the 5 June 1944 airborne landings. (Mike Verier)

During 422 days of combat in six countries the 82nd established a record quite unsurpassed in the US Army, its high casualty rate testimony to the way its masters threw it at the most difficult jobs. The 82nd alone could not of course win wars, what it did better than anybody else, was spearhead, breaching defences and taking on the most difficult opponents so that those who followed could complete the task.

What it also achieved was to influence the Army for a generation. The 82nd produced more generals and senior officers in WWII than any other division, proving that the best officers were indeed attracted to the Airborne. Post-war many other famous commanders would have their roots in service with the Airborne. The division also did more than any other to break down racial barriers and prejudice within the Army. The title 'All Americans' is one it is justly proud of.

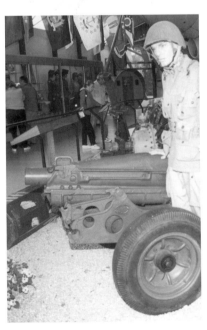

REFERENCE

MUSEUMS

82nd Airborne & Special Operations Museum Foundation
PO Box 89, Fayetteville, NC 28302.
A brand new and very impressive museum sited just outside Fort Bragg in Fayetteville itself. The standard of the exhibits is extremely high. Covering the whole Airborne field it has one of (if not the) best restored CG-4As as well as more modern equipment. Website: www.asomf.org/

82nd Airborne Division War Memorial Museum Fort Bragg, North Carolina.
The division's own museum is sited in the heart of Fort Bragg. It has an impressive collection of equipment and memorabilia. There are also extensive archives for the serious student and a shop. Displayed outside are some artillery pieces and aircraft used by the division ranging from the C-46 to the Huey helicopter. Website: www.bragg.army.mil/rbc/training/82mus

JFK Special Warfare Museum Fort Bragg, North Carolina.
Also sited on Fort Bragg the JFK focuses on special operations from WWII to the present.

General William C. Lee Airborne Museum
209 West Divine Street, PO Box 1111, Dunn, NC 28334
Housed in the former home of General Lee, the museum charts the life and achievements of the man often referred to as the 'Father' of the Airborne.

Museum of Army Flying
Middle Wallop, Hampshire, England
Sited on an operational British Army airfield this museum has a fascinating collection of aircraft, including many rare prototypes and all the gliders used by the Allies. A complete CG-4 and Horsa are on display as is the fuselage and one wing of the world's only surviving Hamilcar. An extensive library is also maintained. At the time of writing restoration of a Hotspur glider is also underway.

INTERNET SITES

www.bragg.army.mil/www-82dv/
82nd Airborne home page with history and individual unit links.

www.army.mil/cmh-pg/
US Army Center of Military History: large section on the 82nd.

www.fayettevillenc.com/airborne82dassn/
Official site of the 82nd Airborne Division Association which is chartered by Congress. It has chapters around the US—such as that in Washington, www.sy-dc.com/82nd/

www.quorndon-mag.org.uk/82nd-airborne/
Friends of the 82nd Airborne Division Association who help people trying to trace information on any servicemen from the 82nd Airborne Division who went through Quorn (Quorndon), prior to D-Day.

www.thedropzone.org/misc/mission.html
On-line virtual museum of airborne subjects.

There are many reenactment sites linked to the division and its units—eg the site of the 82nd Living History Association or that of 2nd Platoon, Fox Company, 505th PIR or D Company 505th PIR (www.mypage.onemain.com/db1014476/db1014476.html, www.foxcompany.org/ and www.dco505pir.fsnet.co.uk/index.html).

www.normandyallies.org/index.htm
Organisation to remember and teach about the US side of D-Day, includes histories of units.

www.army.mil/cmh-pg/matrix/82ABD/82ABD-Decs.htm
82nd Airborne Division Unit Decorations.

www.geocities.com/Pentagon/5340/
504th PIR homepage. Really good site with loads of info and links.

www.csupomona.edu/~rosenkrantz/paratroop/sgtdave.htm
Poignant website to the memory of S/Sgt Dave 'Rosie' Rosenkrantz of the 504th PIR who died in Holland 28 September 1944.

www.nijmegenweb.myweb.nl/
Tribute to the liberators of Nijmegen.

www.marketgarden.f2s.com
The story of Operation Market Garden including details of units and the battles at Nijmegen and Arnhem.

www.triplenickle.com
The excellent website of the 555th Parachute Infantry Association, with photos and historical data on this remarkable unit.

BIBLIOGRAPHY

Ambrose, Stephen E.: *Band of Brothers*; Touchstone, 1992.
A personal account from the perspective of a member of the 506th/101st Division. Again much useful detail on life in the Airborne.

Dawson, Buck: *Saga of the All American*; 82nd Airborne Division Association, 1946.
Published immediately after the war this is an invaluable source. Although the reproduction of the pictures is poor, the content more than makes up. Original reports from soldiers and war correspondents abound and the book covers every campaign in which the 82nd served.

Goldstein, Dilon and Wenger: *Nuts! The Battle of the Bulge*; Brasseys, 1994.
Original pictures are used to illustrate the terrible fighting in the Ardennes. The text is detailed and informative, offering details of the protagonists, the actual fighting and a comparison of the weapons used by the opposing sides.

HQ 52nd Troop Carrier Wing: Secret report 'Operation Market Garden'; USAAF, 1944
A time capsule that details the vast logistic effort needed to get the troops and their supplies to the battlefield.

Kershaw, Robert: *D-Day—Piercing the Atlantic Wall*; Ian Allan Publishing, 1993.
Excellent all-round examination of the invasion of France and the German defence.

McKenzie, John: *The All Americans. The 82nd Airborne*; David & Charles, 1998.
A personal account of one man's war with the 82nd's artillery. It is written with considerable skill and observation, both of the individual events affecting the author directly, and the overall narrative of the division's progress. Descriptions of both glider-borne and parachute combats are vivid, while a good deal of more personal detail of the men and conditions of the day adds substance to the whole. As a senior NCO the author was ideally placed between officers and other ranks to observe and record a very balanced account of life in the Airborne.

Thompson, Leroy: *On time, on target*; Presidio, 2000.
This book offers a detailed overview of the 82nd from its inception to the late eighties. As such it is thorough if a little brief in some areas, but on the whole this is a very readable and workmanlike account written by a noted authority on the subject.

Arnold, James R.: *Campaign 5—Ardennes*; Osprey, 1990.
Badsey, Stephen: *Campaign 24—Arnhem*; Osprey, 1993.
Kemp, Anthony: *Allied Commanders of WWII*; Osprey, 1982.
Quarrie, Bruce: *Order of Battle 5—The Ardennes Offensive V & XVIII US Corps*; Osprey, 1999, 2000.
Rottman and Volstad: *Elite 31—US Army Airborne 1940–90*; Osprey, 1990.
Smith, Carl: *Warrior 26—US Paratrooper 1941–45*; Osprey, 2000.
Osprey's handy guides to uniforms, equipment and organisation are invariably worth examination, and this collection makes a fine starting point for a more detailed examination of the division.

INDEX